Hilary Read

The ass... uide

Gaining a qual...
in assessment i...

READ ON
PUBLICATIONS LTD

Published in 2011 by
Read On Publications Limited
PO Box 162
Bideford
EX39 9DP

Reprinted in 2011

ISBN 978 1 8726 7826 9

Acknowledgements

Thanks to Jessica Ball, Sally Garbett and John Skipworth for their contributions to this book.

Photography by James Barke, Bristol

Graphic Design by Eatcake Design, Bristol

Edited by Sarah Chapman, Bristol

Printed by Toptown Printers Limited, Barnstaple

The Best Assessor's Guide is a redesigned, up-to-date version of *Excellence in assessing* (H. Read, 2006). Updates include: links to the National Occupational Standards and to the new qualifications; new chapters on the qualifications themselves (what's different about them and how to choose the right one); additional assessment methods; and recognising prior learning (RPL). Quotes and examples have also been updated, and new material has been added to reflect recent changes.

Other books by Hilary Read

Excellence in assessment and verification
Excellence in initial assessment
Excellence in reviewing learners' progress
Excellence in assessing
Excellence in planning and delivering learning
Excellence in verifying

These are available from
Read On Publications Limited
PO Box 162
Bideford
EX39 9DP

To order by phone, ring the orderline on 0844 888 7138

Contents

Foreword

Vocational training has always played a vital part in developing the knowledge, skills and abilities of people who choose to learn through work. These learners may be on funded training programmes or on one of their employer's development programmes, or simply among the millions of people, regardless of age or academic ability, who learn through work, with formal and informal input from others.

Assessors have a pivotal role in monitoring, supporting and developing standards of performance within the workforce. Many employers in both the public and private sectors measure staff against performance indicators or national occupational standards. Sometimes these measures result in qualifications, but more frequently their purpose is simply to improve employees' ability to maintain standards in their job roles. Until now, assessors could achieve nationally recognised qualifications only if they were involved in the assessment of National Vocational Qualifications (NVQs), but the newly developed qualifications for assessors have embraced the assessment of all competence and knowledge demonstrated through both performance and understanding, whether it results in a qualification or not.

The challenge we face is how to develop our assessors' ability, skills and confidence. For too long assessors have been regarded as 'the poor relation' in learning and development, instead of the crucial link between theory and its practical application. One of the reasons for this may be that the previous assessor qualifications did not contain robust and explicit knowledge units. The four new qualifications each have a knowledge unit linked to learning and development theories, so that assessors can now gain the knowledge as well as the skills they need.

With degrees becoming more costly, many individuals will opt to learn and gain qualifications through work. The new assessor qualifications have thus come at a time when an ever-increasing range of sectors is embracing vocational learning. All new and existing assessors and those responsible for their development now need to understand the qualifications and choose the right one for their role.

This practitioners' guide has contributions and advice from those involved in the development of the new qualifications, as well as from experienced assessors, employers and trainers. It has been produced by Hilary Read, author of the highly successful *Excellence in...* series of books, which supported assessors and verifiers through their previous qualifications. Hilary's guides have been widely used by assessors working for employers, FE colleges, national and local training providers, the armed forces, the fire service and the NHS. This new guide is a welcome resource for all new and practising assessors: it contains the advice and good practice we use ourselves, and we warmly recommend it to you.

Sally Garbett,
assessor trainer

Bridget Herniman,
work-based
learning consultant
and practitioner

Rob Martin,
assessor trainer,
Harambee Training

3

Introduction

Welcome to *The best assessor's guide*, which contains all the information you need in order to become the best assessor you can be. The purpose of assessment is to ensure that an individual is competent to undertake the responsibilities and perform the activities required by their job, according to the standard for their industry. The best assessors have confidence in their ability to reach an assessment decision and can explain their reasons for doing so – including the methods they have used and the kinds of evidence they have assessed. They also know about the broader picture – what assessment is for and the methods to use.

Assessment is an important part of the teaching–learning process at all levels of education. In the work-based learning sector, assessment plays a key role in every learner's programme, which means that the knowledge and competence of the assessor is crucial for encouraging learners to succeed.

Because you are responsible for judging the performance of learners, you need to make sure that your assessments are sound. It is thus vital for you to develop your expertise, becoming familiar with all aspects of the assessment process so that you can make fair and accurate assessment decisions. This includes understanding the many different methods of assessment and how to use them, as well as their advantages and limitations.

This comprehensive but easy-to-use handbook is for everyone with responsibility for assessing, whether you are new to the role or experienced. You might be:

- an assessor who already holds A1 and V1, and/or the D32 and D33 qualifications
- new to assessment, and needing to gain one of the new qualifications
- responsible for developing staff in assessing.

The handbook will guide you through all aspects of assessment, from the early planning stage to making final assessment decisions. The guide is based on best practice in assessment, and will help to equip you with the skills you need as you develop your role as an assessor.

The guide will enable you to gain the necessary knowledge and skill to achieve one of the new qualifications for assessors, described on pages 9–14.

What's in the guide?

For ease of use, the guide is divided into two main sections. In part one, called *Process and practice*, you will find help with:

- assessor qualifications: what they are, who should take them, and how to choose the right one for you

- who does what in relation to assessing and quality-assuring assessment

- understanding the essential steps in the assessment process: planning, methods of assessment, carrying out assessment, and recording

- how to explain and record your decisions, and give feedback to the learner

- the law and what this means for assessment practice

- keeping up to date with assessment practice.

Part two, called *The assessment methods toolkit*, tells you in more detail about different assessment methods, and includes help with:

- the correct method to use in a given context

- the stages involved for each method

- how to carry it out

- how to record and assess the evidence for the method you used.

You will also find links to the national occupational standards for assessing learner achievement and the assessor qualifications, where appropriate. Throughout the guide are hints, tips, key points and activities to test your knowledge, along with real-life commentaries and examples of assessment practice.

Part 1

Process and practice

This section of the handbook tells you about:

- assessor qualifications, and how to choose the right one for you

- who does what in relation to assessing and quality-assuring assessment

- the essential steps in the assessment process: planning, methods of assessment, carrying out assessment, recording, and giving feedback to the learner

- current legislation relevant to your assessment practice

- keeping up to date with assessment practice.

Activity: Getting the most from part 1

Answer the following questions concerning your skills and knowledge as an assessor.

Questions	Yes	No	Not sure	Turn to pages
1 Do you know which assessor qualification you need to gain?	☐	☐	☐	9–14
2 Do you know about who does what in relation to regulation, awarding, assessing, and internal and external quality assuring of qualifications?	☐	☐	☐	15–20
3 Can you describe the process of assessment, and say where it fits in with learning and development?	☐	☐	☐	21–4
4 Do you know how to plan for assessment?	☐	☐	☐	25–30
5 Do you know what the different assessment methods are and what they are used for?	☐	☐	☐	32–3
6 Can you reach a safe assessment decision?	☐	☐	☐	33–4
7 Do you know how to give feedback to learners on their performance?	☐	☐	☐	34–5
8 Do you know the legal position with regard to assessing?	☐	☐	☐	39–46
9 Do you know how to use reflective practice as part of your continuing professional development (CPD)?	☐	☐	☐	47–52

Where you have answered no or not sure, turn to the relevant pages of the guide first.

Qualifications
for assessors

New qualifications for assessors have been developed in the Qualifications and Credit Framework (QCF). Based on new occupational standards, the new qualifications now have a single unit devoted to knowledge, containing vital information about the principles and practice of good-quality assessment. The other units reflect the different roles much better than the previous qualifications, and offer increased flexibility in the way vocational achievement can be assessed and demonstrated. There is a unit for those who work with learners who perform in the working environment, and a unit for those who work with learners to assess their vocational skills and knowledge (through assignments, for example) in a non-work environment. Assessors who do both can undertake both these units.

This section describes the three units that, in different combinations, comprise the qualifications aimed at assessors, and will help you choose the right one according to your role. You will find information and advice about:

- the Qualifications and Credit Framework

- why we have new qualifications

- how the new qualifications are structured and who should take them

- where the new qualifications fit within the QCF

- the differences between the new and old qualifications

- choosing the right qualification for you.

The Qualifications and Credit Framework (QCF)

From January 2011 all new qualifications are within the framework, and all new candidates will have to register for these qualifications under the QCF. The new assessor and quality-assurance qualifications have been written with this in mind.

There are eight levels within the QCF, from Entry Level to Level 8, and these describe the level of difficulty or challenge. For example, A Levels are the equivalent of Level 3 and a PhD is equivalent to level 8.

There are also three types of qualification: Award, Certificate and Diploma. These are made up of units, each of which has a number of credits that go to make up the qualification. The new qualifications for assessment and quality assurance are available as awards and certificates.

All qualifications in the QCF have a credit value. Each credit represents approximately ten hours, so that the number of credits awarded for each qualification shows how long it might take to complete. The more credits a qualification has, the more hours are involved.

Overall credit values are as follows:

- Award: 1–12 credits
- Certificate: 13–36 credits.
- Diploma: 37 credits or above.

The terms Award, Certificate and Diploma describe the size of the qualification and how long it takes to achieve.

It looks like this:

Within the QCF, there is scope for flexibility and tailoring qualifications to your individual needs. For example, an award at level 7 is a small qualification at a high level, whereas a diploma at level 2 is a larger qualification but at a lower level. It is possible to gain both an award at level 7 and a diploma at level 2.

Units within the QCF are structured in the same way. Each contains the following:

- **unit title:** this tells you what the unit is about

- **level:** this describes the level of difficulty

- **credit value:** this tells you how many credits the unit is worth

- **learning outcomes:** these tell you what you are expected to know, understand or be able to do

- **assessment criteria:** these specify the standard you must meet to show that you have achieved the learning outcome.

The credit value tells you the average time it takes to achieve the learning outcomes and assessment criteria within each unit. Learning time means more than just the guided learning hours: it includes everything you have to do to achieve the unit, such as practising within your workplace or working through a self-study workbook on your own. One credit is equal to approximately ten hours' learning time, so that if you were taking a unit worth six credits, it would take you an average of 60 hours to achieve.

Why do we have new qualifications for assessors?

New qualifications are needed to fit within the Qualifications and Curriculum Framework (QCF) and to reflect changes in the practices of assessment and quality assurance. The new qualifications have been developed as a result of the revised national occupational standards (NOS) for learning and development, following wide consultation within the sector. The new standards reflect current practice in learning and development, and describe what a person needs to do, know and understand in order to carry out their learning and development role in a consistent and competent way.

Who needs the qualifications?

The QCF becomes fully operational at the beginning of 2011, but existing NVQs will continue to operate for three more years, to allow learners who are already registered to complete them. If you are already an assessor and do not have the A, V or D units, you will need to achieve one of the new qualifications. If you are new to assessing, then the implications are as follows:

- If you deliver these existing qualifications, you still need to be qualified to meet both the requirements of the NVQ Code of Practice and your Sector Skills Council's (SSC's) assessment strategies.

- If you deliver QCF qualifications with 'NVQ' in the title, you will also need to gain one of the qualifications.

- Depending on what your Sector Skills Council specifies within the relevant assessment strategy, you may need to gain a new qualification if you assess or quality assure qualifications that don't have NVQ in their titles, where you are responsible for confirming occupational competence.

- If you already hold an existing qualification (the A, V or D units), you do not have to requalify, but you must be aware of the new standards and able to show that your knowledge and practice are in accordance with the relevant new qualification. This may mean undergoing additional continual professional development (CPD).

The new qualifications at a glance

Four qualifications are aimed at assessors. Three of them are awards and the fourth is a certificate. Each qualification includes a unit covering the essential knowledge and understanding that assessors need, plus one or more units that are about competent practice. If you are new to assessment, this means you can choose to take the knowledge unit and gain an understanding of assessment or quality assurance principles and practice before you begin practising within a role, then go on to take further units when you are ready to begin. Equally, if you are ready to carry out real assessment with real learners, then you can undertake both the knowledge and applied units at the same time and take a holistic approach using the same evidence: it's up to you.

Level 3 Award in Understanding the Principles and Practices of Assessment
This award consists of a knowledge-based unit and is aimed at those wanting to gain an understanding without the need to practise

Unit 1:
Understanding the Principles and Practices of Assessment

Level 3 Award in Assessing Competence in the Work Environment
This award is for assessors who assess occupational competence using naturally occurring evidence from work

Unit 1: Understanding the Principles and Practices of Assessment	**Unit 2:** Assess Occupational Competence in the Work Environment

Level 3 Award in Assessing Vocationally Related Achievement
This award is for assessors who assess vocational skills, knowledge and understanding in other environments

Unit 1: Understanding the Principles and Practices of Assessment	**Unit 3:** Assess Vocational Skills, Knowledge and Understanding

Level 3 Certificate in Assessing Vocational Achievement
The certificate is for assessors who do both

Unit 1: Understanding the Principles and Practices of Assessment	**Unit 2:** Assess Occupational Competence in the Work Environment	**Unit 3:** Assess Vocational Skills, Knowledge and Understanding

Credit values of the new qualifications

Qualification	QCF level	Credits
Award in Understanding the Principles and Practices of Assessment	3	3
Award in Assessing Competence in the Work Environment	3	9
Award in Assessing Vocationally Related Achievement	3	9
Certificate in Assessing Vocational Achievement	3	15

What are the main differences between the old and new qualifications?

The new qualifications are not the same as the A1 and V1 awards. They have a different structure and use some new terminology. Here is a summary of the main differences between these and previous assessor and IQA (verifier) qualifications:

What's different about the new qualifications?	Why's that?
Verification is now called quality assurance (internal or external).	To underline the key purpose of the role: whereas verification of assessment is only part of the responsibility, quality assurance is the overall requirement.
Each set of qualifications now has a knowledge unit.	To ensure that there is a formal input on the main principles and practices of assessment and internal and external quality assurance when people are being trained and developed. The knowledge unit can be taken before someone takes on the role, allowing for pre-service development, by those who are 'just looking' or by those who want to understand what's involved.
You will no longer find Common Agreed Evidence Requirements between awarding organisations offering the new qualifications. There are, however, clear guidelines for assessment methods, acceptable evidence and the qualifications and experience of those who assess and quality assure the new qualifications.[1]	To allow more options when it comes to presenting evidence of competence (you may find this a challenge if you are used to being given prescriptive definitions as to what constitutes acceptable evidence).
There are no elements and performance criteria.	To comply with the QCF: the new qualifications contain learning outcomes and assessment criteria instead.

[1] See *Assessing and Assuring the Quality of Assessment: Guidance for awarding organisations*, LLUK, March 2010

Activity: Choosing the right qualification

This activity will help you choose the qualification that is right for your role.
Answer yes or no to the following questions:

Do you...	Yes	No	Not sure
a assess mainly in the work environment?	☐	☐	☐
b mainly use methods such as observation of performance, questioning or discussing with the learner?	☐	☐	☐
c assess mainly in other environments such as the workshop, training room or classroom?	☐	☐	☐
d mainly use methods such as simulations, skills tests, assignments, projects and/or case studies?	☐	☐	☐
e assess in both the work environment and the workshop or classroom environments?	☐	☐	☐
f assess using most or all of the methods under b) and d) above?	☐	☐	☐
g need to find out more about the principles and practices of assessment (and aren't currently practising)?	☐	☐	☐

If you answered yes to a) and b) you need to take the Level 3 Award in Assessing Competence in the Work Environment.

If you answered yes to c) and d) you need to take the Level 3 Award in Assessing Vocationally Related Achievement.

If you answered yes to a) – f) you need to take the Level 3 Certificate in Assessing Vocational Achievement, especially if you envisage assessing new assessors as part of your role.

If you answered yes to e) and f) you need to take the Level 3 Certificate in Assessing Vocational Achievement.

If you answered yes only to g) you need to take the Level 3 Award in Understanding the Principles and Practices of assessment.

If you answered 'not sure' to one or more, or your answers are inconclusive you may need to redo the activity with the help of a more senior colleague, such as your IQA or centre manager.

Key point

It's not the context within which you assess that dictates the qualification you need, but the assessment methods you use. If the methods you use cut across both of the applied units, consider taking the Certificate in Assessing Vocational Achievement.

Who does what
in assessment

This section goes into more detail concerning who does what during the process of assessing vocational qualifications or national occupational standards (NOS). You will be able to see clearly where you as an assessor fit within the system for delivering qualifications and assessment. Here you will find information on:

- who's who in delivery

- the assessor's main responsibilities

- the main responsibilities of internal quality assurers

- the main responsibilities of external quality assurers.

Who's who in delivery

Here's an overview of all those involved in the delivery of qualifications and assessment.

Office of the Qualifications and Examinations Regulator (Ofqual), Council for the Curriculum, Examinations and Assessment (CCEA), Department for Children, Education, Lifelong Learning and Skills (DCELLS)
The qualifications regulatory bodies responsible for overseeing national qualifications, examinations and assessments in England, and vocational qualifications in Northern Ireland and Wales.

Standards Setting Body (SSB) or Sector Skills Council (SSC)
Organisations responsible for developing national occupational standards and qualifications.

Qualifications and Credit Framework (QCF)
One of the frameworks for creating and accrediting qualifications in England, Wales and Northern Ireland.

Awarding organisations
Organisations approved by the qualifications regulatory bodies to award qualifications. All learners register for a qualification with an awarding organisation and are awarded credits upon successful completion.

External quality assurer (EQA)
The person appointed by the awarding organisation to monitor the work of the approved centre. The EQA acts as the link between the awarding organisation and the approved centre by working closely with the internal quality assurers and centre manager to ensure that the quality of assessment and internal quality assurance meets the national standard.

THE APPROVED ASSESSMENT CENTRE (MANAGED BY A CENTRE CO-ORDINATOR OR MANAGER)

Internal quality assurer (IQA)
The person appointed by the approved centre responsible for ensuring the quality and consistency of the assessment process.

Assessor
This is you, the person appointed by the approved centre and responsible for working with the learner to advise and assess them.

Candidates/learners
Individuals registered with an awarding organisation and working towards achieving the units/qualifications.

The assessor's main responsibilities

As the assessor, you are responsible for deciding whether or not your learners have achieved the relevant standards. The following are your main areas of responsibility, and what you need to know within those areas.

You are responsible for...	You need to know...
• assessing learners' knowledge, understanding and skills against assessment criteria in a real-life work environment and/or under simulated conditions, or in a classroom or workshop	• the subject or occupation you are assessing and how to reach assessment decisions that are valid, fair and reliable
• choosing and using appropriate assessment methods at the right time and in the right combinations (see 'Assessment methods to use' below)	• different assessment methods and when to use them • how to plan assessment • holistic approaches to assessing based on the learner's activities
• giving feedback to learners	• how you involve the learner (and others, such as the employer or the learner's supervisor) in the assessment process
• recording assessment decisions	• how to manage information relating to assessment
• carrying out best practice with regard to assessment	• how to use activity-based, cost-effective, non-bureaucratic, (holistic) assessment, where appropriate • centre policies such as dealing with disputes and appeals, confidentiality, health and safety, equality and diversity, and safeguarding • knowing the value of reflective practice and continuing professional development within your own professional practice
• contributing to the quality assurance of assessment.	• standardisation methods and procedures.

'I am a peripatetic assessor and standardisation meetings are particularly important for us, as we mostly work in isolation.'

Assessment methods to use

In the work environment

• observation of performance

• examining work products

• questioning the learner

• discussing with the learner

• looking at learner statements

• recognising prior learning.

In other environments

• assessing the learner in simulated environments

• skills tests

• oral and written questions

• assignments

• projects

• case studies

• recognising prior learning.

The main responsibilities of internal quality assurers

Internal quality assurers (IQAs) are responsible for maintaining and improving assessment within your centre. Their job is to ensure that procedures are in place to support you in making a robust and reliable assessment decision each time you assess.

IQAs are responsible for...	They need to know...
• ensuring and improving the quality of assessment within centres	• how to sample evidence of assessment and assessment processes
	• how to use appropriate criteria for judging the quality of the assessment process.
• planning how IQA will take place	• ways of maintaining and improving the quality of assessment, using standardisation procedures, for example
	• how to ensure that assessors have the right competence and expertise to carry out their roles.
• carrying out good practice for the internal quality assurance of assessment	• the impact of legal issues, including health, safety and welfare of others
• keeping up to date with current practice	• the requirements for equality and diversity
	• how continuing professional development and reflective practice contribute to improvements in IQA.
• recording the results of IQA	• how to apply centre procedures for managing information (recording, storing and reporting, including maintaining confidentiality).
• giving feedback, advice and support to assessors to enable them to maintain the quality of assessment and improve on their performance.	• ways of standardising assessment practice such as observing assessors in action, standardisation meetings and peer review.

'Any IQA responsible for a team should have an appreciation of their assessors' workloads and ability to deliver. For example, funded qualifications often mean meeting targets by specified deadlines, and this can lead to assessors being given unrealistic workloads if they are poorly managed.'

If IQAs are responsible for a team, they are also responsible for:	This means they need to know about...
• recruiting staff	• meeting the requirements of their centre
	• equality and diversity, and safeguarding issues
• staffing levels and structures	• the centre's legal obligations and the workload of assessors.
• meeting with the EQA and ensuring that their recommendations are implemented	• the awarding organisation's requirements
• staff development.	• ways of managing performance and carrying out staff appraisals.

The main responsibilities of external quality assurers

External quality assurers (EQAs) are normally appointed by awarding organisations. EQAs are responsible for ensuring that assessment and internal quality assurance are carried out consistently across a number of centres.

EQAs are responsible for...	They need to know...
• maintaining and improving the quality of internal quality assurance across a number of centres	• how to evaluate externally the quality of assessment and internal quality assurance, using techniques such as sampling
• planning how EQA will take place	• how to plan and carry out external quality visits to centres
	• legal and good practice requirements
• monitoring and critically evaluating the quality of the centre's:	
◦ IQA systems	
◦ administrative arrangements	
◦ staffing levels and staff expertise and competence	
◦ arrangements for assessment, the methods used and the assessment decisions made	
• providing advice and support to centres.	• ways of giving feedback and support to centres.

What the standards say

National occupational standards (NOS) Standard 9: Assess learner achievement	
Performance criteria	**Knowledge and understanding**
9.1 Ensure learners understand the purpose, requirements and processes of assessment	**KU1** The key concepts and principles of assessment

Assessor units		
Unit title	**Learning outcomes**	**Assessment criteria**
1 Understanding the principles and practices of assessment	**1** Understand the principles and requirements of assessment	**1.3** Explain the responsibilities of the assessor

Assessment and internal quality assurance

A reliable system of assessment and internal quality assurance will help to ensure that you are delivering training and accrediting qualifications in line with national standards and regulations, and enabling learners to be successful in achieving their chosen qualifications. Assessors and IQAs therefore play a key role in assessing learning and helping learners to progress, while ensuring that national standards are maintained. As an assessor, you need to be clear about the part you play in enabling learners to succeed.

This section tells you about:

- the stages in the assessment process
- the stages in the internal quality assurance process.

The assessment process

Knowing when to assess is vital. It is expensive to assess learners before they have acquired the necessary skills and knowledge to perform consistently to the standards. It is therefore important that you know exactly how your individual learners are progressing, so that you can plan for assessment at the right time.

When you look at how learning and assessment are delivered, you can see how closely the two are linked, as follows:

Stage	Learning and development	Assessment
1 Recruitment	The learner is recruited to the programme.	The learner undergoes initial assessment to: • assess their potential • see what they can do already • gauge their suitability and is then registered with the awarding organisation.
2 Induction	The learner is inducted into their learning and development programme.	The learner is inducted into the qualification and assessment process.
3 Planning for learning and assessment for learning	The learner agrees learning targets, and plans are made for how these will be achieved. These are recorded on an individual learning plan (ILP), or similar.	The results of initial assessment inform plans and ensure that realistic targets are set. Regular assessment for learning is planned.
4 Learning and development	The learner undergoes training and development over time and: • acquires skills and knowledge • practises and applies what they have learned • starts to perform to the standards • consistently performs to the standards under a variety of conditions at work.	Assessment for learning takes place at regular intervals to see how the learner is progressing. Learners are given feedback on their performance, targets are adjusted and further training and development are arranged as necessary. When (and *only* when) the learner is performing confidently and consistently to appropriate standards …
5 Assessment planning		… does planning for assessment against the standards take place. This is where the learner agrees an assessment plan – how, when and where assessment will take place – with their assessor.
6 Assessment against the standards	If the learner is assessed as 'not yet competent', they may need to undertake further training or practice.	The assessor makes an assessment decision and gives feedback to the learner on their performance. Further assessment is planned as necessary.
7 Certification		The learner receives a certificate of their achievement from the relevant awarding organisation.

The internal quality assurance process

Ultimately, it is the IQA's job to ensure the integrity and quality of assessment, so he or she must make sure that effective procedures and resources are in place to allow this to happen.

As an assessor, you have an important part to play in maintaining the quality of assessment within your centre. Your IQA will ask you to participate in meetings and activities that maintain and improve the quality of the assessment process, including observing your practice.

Here's how the internal quality assurance process supports the delivery of assessment:

Stage	The IQA...	The assessor...
1	maintains policies and procedures to enable and improve the delivery of assessment. trains and supports assessors in their use.	
2	internally quality assures assessment, by sampling the work of assessors and learners and observing assessors' performance.	plans and carries out assessment with learners.
3	evaluates the effectiveness of assessment practice and procedures.	actively contributes to quality assurance, for example during team and standardisation meetings.
4	modifies practice and procedures as a result of evaluation. produces individual development plans for each assessor, based on observations and sampling of his or her work. supports assessors in implementing changes.	modifies his or her assessment practice, and undergoes further training and development as necessary.

'Only the assessor can judge whether or not the learner has met the standards. You can't take another person's say-so and signature on an account of a learner's competence without checking – otherwise you wouldn't need the assessor.'

What the standards say

National occupational standards (NOS) Standard 9: Assess learner achievement	
Performance criteria	**Knowledge and understanding**
9.8 Work with others to ensure the standardisation of assessment practice and outcomes	**KU18** How to co-operate and work effectively with others involved in the assessment process

Assessor units	
Unit title	**Learning outcomes**
1 Understanding the principles and practices of assessment	**6** Understand quality assurance of the assessment process

Assessment planning

Before you begin to assess a learner, you will need to make a plan of how you will carry out your assessment. Your overall aim is to plan for the types of evidence you will need to see to inform your assessment decision and next steps. The way in which you plan should reflect a holistic approach to assessment. This means planning assessment around what the learner is doing, then linking these activities to the standards, and not the other way round. This is particularly important for learners in the working environment.

This section explains:

- the principles of holistic planning
- how to plan for holistic assessment with your learners
- the best way to make a holistic assessment plan, with an example of how to record assessment.

The principles of holistic planning

- Start from the key activities the learner does at work, or a work activity that is coming up.

- Make a separate assessment plan for each assessment episode or visit.

- Think of assessment planning as an iterative process: this means you base subsequent plans on what happens as a result of the previous one.

Initial planning with learners

The first phase of the assessment planning process happens when the learner is first recruited to a programme leading to a vocational qualification. Ideally, all assessors should play a part in recruiting the right learner. You will need to be sure that the learner's job, the results of initial assessment, and their aptitudes and attainments indicate that they are likely to succeed in the qualification they have chosen. If you don't do this, you risk setting the learner up for disappointment or failure. Most learners will 'vote with their feet' and leave their programme if they cannot succeed, and so if you think this will happen it is best to recommend at the earliest possible stage that the learner not be recruited to, or continue with, their programme.

Having recruited the learner, your job at the initial planning stage is to help them gain an overview of the qualification they are hoping to achieve and to plan their route to achieving it. This may involve helping them select the right units in the right order, and identifying any extra support they might need.

Remember

The assessor qualifications are structured so that each has a knowledge unit and applied units. The context and methods are different, but by carrying out the applied unit you also cover the knowledge unit.

You will find the following steps useful when planning assessment with learners in the early stages:

1 Before you start, make sure you have an overview of all the relevant units within the learner's chosen path. You also need to take account of the results of your initial assessment of the learner. Make sure, too, that you have all the necessary documents to hand concerning the learner's existing achievements and their potential.

2 Gauge the level at which the learner is currently working. If they are expecting to take the qualification at a different level, you will need to explain how their learning and development will be designed to get them to the appropriate level for them.

3 If you are assessing in the work environment, identify what the learner does on a day-to-day basis, listing their main functions and responsibilities, then try and group these into key activities.

4 Now link the units in the qualification to these key activities.

5 Next, identify any specialist activities that the learner carries out. Focus on the units where these occur. You will usually find that the generic competencies that underpin most of what the learner does also occur naturally when they carry out their specialist activities. Group these units and/or learning outcomes together because you will be assessing them together. This is the essence of holistic planning.

6 Find out whether the learner has any particular assessment requirements, such as working shifts or part-time hours, or any physical and practical needs, which may mean making special arrangements.

> **Tip**
>
> Aim to use a minimum of three assessment methods and/or types of evidence from each assessment episode, as this stops you relying too much on one method.

Recording the assessment plan

Each assessment plan should include:

- who is being assessed, where and when

- what activity is being assessed, and the units for which evidence will be provided

- what assessment methods will be used, how they will be recorded, and where the evidence will be stored after the assessment

- when and how feedback will be given

- who else needs to be informed of, or involved in, the assessment (especially if you are using someone else to confirm the learner's performance)

- what the arrangements are for reviewing progress and updating arrangements for assessment

- anything the learner needs to bring on the day of assessment (particularly if you are using discussion to provide evidence of a task or activity you have not observed).

Your awarding organisation must approve the documentation you use to record your assessment plans, and you need to follow your centre's procedures when filling it in.

Example assessment plan

The following example of an assessment plan is based on the Certificate in Assessing Vocational Achievement. The completed assessment record made as a result of this plan is on pages 58–9.

Assessment plan

Learner assessor	Assessor	Qualification
Stephen Jackson	Ameera Patel	L3 Certificate in assessing vocational achievement

Location of assessment	Date of assessment	
Peters & Wright Estate Agents	23 and 26 June 2011	

Activity to be assessed	Evidence to be judged	Assessment method	Unit
Stephen observing his learner, dealing with clients at work. Stephen's assessment of his learner's assignment	PERFORMANCE EVIDENCE: Observing and questioning the learner; questioning the client (witness). Assessment of assignment and Stephen's questioning of his learner in relation to the completed assignment.	Observation	1,2,3 2
Stephen providing feedback to his learner	PERFORMANCE EVIDENCE: Providing feedback, questioning learner, planning next steps with learner.	Observation	1,2,3
Completed assessment records and documentation	PRODUCT EVIDENCE: Completed assessment records, including observation report; judgment and assessment decision; summary of feedback and evidence location sheet.	Examining products of work	1,2,3
Stephen's knowledge and understanding of the assessment process and underpinning theories	KNOWLEDGE EVIDENCE: Principles and requirements of evidence. Factors when planning assessment and use of different methods. Factors in making assessment decisions. How questioning and feedback contribute to assessment.	Discussion and questioning via Skype	1

The planning process starts here with the main activities Stephen will be carrying out at work as an assessor

This column contains the main methods of assessment to be used when assessing Stephen

Notice how each activity covers more than one unit

This column specifies the evidence Stephen will produce

Remote technology is being used here to fit the discussion around Stephen's and his assessor's work schedules.

Stephen knows what is expected from him when he discusses his performance as an assessor.

Key considerations for holistic assessment planning

- Consider ways of involving your learner's line manager or employer in planning for assessment, as they are usually the best person to tell you about the learner's work schedule.

- Think of *all* the likely evidence that might be covered in a single assessment episode. For example, a simple activity, such as cutting a client's hair, could also provide other evidence for customer service, handling equipment and resources, working relationships, and health and safety.

- Check that your learner knows about, and is prepared for, the assessment methods you plan to use. For example, they will need to prepare for a discussion in advance, and will need to know what you will be covering if you are going to question them.

- If you think you will need additional performance evidence, plan for the best ways to identify and capture this. For example, it might need to be in written form from another person (a witness) or in the form of a discussion with the employer.

What the standards say

National occupational standards (NOS) Standard 9: Assess learner achievement	
Performance criteria	**Knowledge and understanding**
9.2 Plan assessment to meet requirements and learner needs	**KU5** Guidelines for assessment planning as appropriate to own area of responsibility

Assessor units		
Unit title	**Learning outcomes**	**Assessment criteria**
2 Assess occupational competence in the work environment	**1** Be able to plan the assessment of occupational competence	**1.1** Plan assessment of occupational competence based on the following methods:
		1.2 Communicate the purpose, requirements and processes of assessing occupational competence to the learner
		1.3 Plan the assessment of occupational competence to address learner needs and current achievements
		1.4 Identify opportunities for holistic assessment

Carrying out assessment

Broadly, you will be carrying out assessment to find out, in a systematic and objective way, whether your learners are performing against the standards for which you are assessing. At the same time you are using assessment as a tool to influence future learning, because it should enable you to explore and identify what aspects of their job or learning programme the learner finds challenging and the skills they need to improve. Best practice in assessment should empower learners by allowing them to see their achievements, and motivate them to make progress by enabling them to understand where and how they need to develop further.

This section looks at all aspects of carrying out assessment with learners, and tells you how to:

- use different assessment methods

- make sound assessment decisions

- give meaningful feedback to learners

- record the results of your assessment.

Using different assessment methods

As an assessor, you need to have confidence in your ability to reach a good assessment decision. The key to making a safe and reliable decision is to use the most appropriate assessment method for the evidence with which you are presented and for the learner's needs and circumstances. You can be flexible and creative in your choice of method, but you must be able to justify its use and any subsequent decision you make.

Your awarding organisation will have specific guidance on the assessment methods to use, so you will also need to find out this information.

The table opposite summarises the main assessment methods, what they mean and when to use them. You will find more detailed help on each of the methods in part two, 'The assessment methods toolkit', on page 53.

Making assessment decisions

By using a range of assessment methods, and choosing the most appropriate one for the purpose, you should be in a position to make firm decisions about the learner's competence against the standards.

Before making your decision, use 'VAS', by asking the following questions:

Is the evidence...	
valid?	Does it meet the learning outcomes and assessment criteria of the standards?
authentic?	Has the learner produced the evidence?
sufficient?	Is there enough evidence to prove that the learner has demonstrated competence over time and under different conditions?

For the learner to meet the standards in question, you must be able to answer yes confidently to each question, and demonstrate to your IQA that you have undertaken this process against every piece of evidence your learner presents to you.

If you answer no to one or more of the above VAS questions, this will tell you that the learner has not yet met the standards.

The main assessment methods

Method	What it means	When to use it
Observation	Watching learners perform in the workplace	To see learners demonstrate their practical skills as they do their job activities. Most standard setting bodies (SSBs) specify observation as a primary or mandatory method within their assessment strategies
Examining work products	The outcomes or products of a learner's work activity	In conjunction with observation, questioning or professional discussion; must be the result of real work
Questioning	Using a range of questioning techniques, either spoken or written	To find out whether a learner has the necessary knowledge
Discussion	A conversation in which learners describe and reflect on their performance and knowledge in relation to the requirements of the standards	To test the validity and reliability of a learner's evidence. Can often be used to cover a range of work activities and units. An effective way to test 'deep' rather than 'superficial' learning
Evidence from others (witness testimony)	Another person's account of what a learner has done, usually to confirm existing knowledge from your own observation	To support an observation and to confirm consistent performance over time. May be used in conjunction with RPL (see below) to verify a learner's claim to existing knowledge and skills
Learner statements	The learner's account of what they have been doing in relation to the standards to be achieved	To support consistent performance over time, or for evidence of reflection on, and improvements in, performance
Projects, assignments and case studies	Assessing the outcomes of case studies, projects and assignments that a learner has undertaken as part of their vocational learning against specified criteria	In conjunction with questioning or discussion. (Remember, though, that projects and assignments set as part of the learning process provide no evidence of competence.)
Simulation	Using a replica of the work environment to assess competence	When it is impossible or unsafe for the learner to perform in a real-life work environment
Skills tests	Formal testing of skills under test conditions	When it forms part of the requirements for independent assessment in certain qualifications, usually those where learners need to acquire a range of technical skills before they can perform in the work environment; or safety-related knowledge and skill requirements
Recognition of prior learning (RPL)	Assessment of a learner's existing level of knowledge and skill in relation to the standards	To match prior learning to units in a qualification so the learner doesn't have to repeat what they have already learned; without detailed assessment, it can be difficult to judge whether prior claims constitute valid, authentic and current evidence

Unreliable evidence

Some of the issues you may have to deal with when reaching a sound assessment decision are to do with the quality of evidence. You may encounter problems with authenticity of evidence, as in the first two of the following quotes, or with evidence that is not current, as in the third quote below. You will have to deal with these issues sensitively but decisively. Don't be afraid to say no to evidence that you feel is unreliable – it's your job to do so.

'I was assessing standards for a range of learners and found some project evidence that was exactly the same in three of the portfolios. They had obviously copied each other's work and just printed it off!'

'One supervisor blatantly told a lie and said that his learner had operated a particular type of machinery on a regular basis, when I knew for a fact that the company did not possess such equipment. On questioning him, he said he thought it wasn't important and that he was doing the learner a favour.'

'I recently had somebody who wanted to submit evidence using the RPL process. They wanted to use the fact that they had achieved G3 from the Learning and Development Standards as evidence that they were improving their performance. I checked to see if they were still evaluating their performance on a regular basis, and they had done nothing since achieving the unit. The evidence was therefore not allowed.'

Giving feedback to learners

Giving feedback to learners on your assessment decisions is an important part of your role. Learners do not know how well they are doing unless you tell them. Effective feedback is the basis on which learners progress, in terms of developing their knowledge and skills and ultimately working to the appropriate standards.

When and how to give feedback

You need to give feedback after each assessment episode. Your aim is to explain the assessment decision(s) to the learner and plan and agree what happens next, in the light of this decision. This means:

- If the learner's evidence meets the assessment criteria, you explain this and plan for the next assessment episode.

- If the learner's evidence does not meet the assessment criteria, you explain why not, and plan for further development or training.

If you are new to giving feedback on performance, you may find the following stages helpful:

1 **Begin by describing the elements of the learner's performance that have met the assessment criteria, using specific examples of what they did.**

   Don't assume that the learner will know what was good without you telling them. You are also more likely to get the learner's attention and motivate them if what you have to say is positive.

2 **Ask the learner to comment on how well they think they did, and encourage them to say what they think they could improve or do differently next time.**

   This helps learners to develop skills of self-assessment. Your skill in giving feedback at this stage is to draw out areas that need improving, through discussion with the learner.

3 **Make suggestions for improvement to the learner.**

At this stage, you are focusing on what will help the learner improve. Use factual descriptions of their performance in relation to the standards, and pinpoint the areas that the learner can change. Allow the learner time to think about these, and to ask questions and comment on what you have said. Aim to share ideas, and offer choices rather than prescribed courses of action.

In summary...

1 **Start with what went well.**

- Tell the learner what they did well and the evidence you saw to support this, even if they did not meet the assessment criteria.

- Treat occasions where the assessment criteria have not been met as opportunities for development; don't talk in terms of mistakes or failures.

2 **Involve the learner.**

- Ask them how they think they did.

- Base your feedback on evidence of what you've seen or heard, not opinion or feelings.

- Give examples of what you mean.

- Allow your learner the opportunity to ask questions.

3 **Be clear about why the learner did or didn't achieve, and say what needs to happen next.**

- Pinpoint specific areas that need to change.

- Say what the learner did or didn't do.

- Explain what they need to do next time.

- Agree targets and record these on the next assessment plan.

Activity: Will my feedback be effective?

Ask yourself the following questions before giving feedback to your learner. You are aiming to answer yes in each case.

Questions	Yes	No
1 Have I told the learner they will be getting feedback, and when?	☐	☐
2 Have I thought about what I am going to say, and how the learner might react?	☐	☐
3 Will I be giving feedback in a private place without interruptions?	☐	☐
4 During the feedback session, will I give the learner an opportunity to comment on his or her own performance and ask questions?	☐	☐
5 Am I sure that the outcome will be an agreed way forward, with clear, achievable objectives for the learner?	☐	☐

Recording assessment decisions

Since it is vital that your assessments are seen to be reliable, valid, objective and fair, you will need to keep formal records of all your assessment decisions so that the process is open and transparent. A record of assessment is a document that describes:

- how the evidence has met the learning outcomes and assessment criteria

- where you saw the evidence, particularly if it was in the workplace

- the assessment methods you used

- the date and time of your assessment.

The important thing is to record your assessment decision – whether or not the assessment criteria were met – against each piece of evidence.

When you assess evidence that is in paper or other material form, it can still be kept wherever it is naturally located, such as in a filing cabinet, desk or workshop. In this case your record of assessment must show the evidence produced, the assessment decision, and where the evidence is kept. This is so that you can explain how you arrived at your assessment decision, if a learner appeals or your IQA asks you.

Tip

It is not necessary to make learners keep copies of all the evidence they produce in one place (such as in a portfolio) as this places unnecessary demands on them, and turns the process of assessment into a bureaucratic one.

What documents do I need?

Most of the items that you need to keep as part of the record of assessment can be included in one or two documents. The items include:

- results of assessment planning (one overall ILP, then ongoing assessment plans)

- products resulting from assessment episodes, such as:

  - observations of performance

  - recorded discussions

  - others' accounts

- your assessment decisions

- the feedback you give to the learner

- any agreed action points arising from assessment.

What goes into the learner's portfolio?

Strictly speaking, there is no need for learners to have a portfolio: if you follow a holistic approach to planning and carrying out assessment, the evidence stays in situ (the place where you assessed it) and the learner doesn't need to collect it in one place. The following list describes what the portfolio should and should not contain.

What goes in the learner's portfolio	What does not go into the portfolio
• A list of assessment decisions	• The learner's CV
• A declaration signed by the learner and you, stating that the evidence and decisions are authentic	• Organisation charts
• Assessment plans	• Organisational policies and procedures
• Recorded assessments detailing what was assessed, the methods you used, the location of the evidence and what was achieved	• Any training and learning materials, such as projects or assignments used for developmental purposes
• Feedback given on performance	• Unit summaries
	• Cross-reference matrices

Since 2006, there has been no requirement for learners and assessors to sign and date every item of evidence (See Code of Practice, Ofqual, 2006). Despite this, it is still common practice in some centres. If you aren't sure, you can save yourself time and trouble by using a declaration like the one below.

The following example of a declaration is for one of the assessor awards.

Remember

A declaration such as the example shown here should be the last item you complete for the assessment.

Level 3 Award in Assessing Competence in the Work Environment

I .... (insert the assessor's name)

and ....(insert the learner's name)

confirm that:

- competence has been demonstrated consistently over a period of time

- evidence provided for assessment has been produced and authenticated in accordance with awarding body requirements

- all evidence presented is valid, authentic and sufficient

- assessment was conducted under the required conditions and contexts

- quality assurance checks have been carried out, ensuring that the learner meets all requirements of the standards and qualification.

Assessor's signature .... Date...................

Learner's signature.. Date...................

Key considerations for carrying out assessment

- Make sure your learner is ready to be assessed. This means that you must be certain that they are already meeting the standards in question; otherwise you are wasting your time or – worse – setting your learner up to fail.

- Remember that it is your job as the assessor to identify the evidence, not the learner's. The learner needs to carry out their work as normal and be prepared to discuss it with you afterwards, as appropriate.

- Think about the best time to give feedback: it doesn't have to be straight after assessing. Instead, it might be better to give it at the end of the working day or after work. Although you should always give feedback at a time and in a form appropriate to the learner, you also need to allow yourself enough time to consider all the evidence.

What the standards say

National occupational standards (NOS) Standard 9: Assess learner achievement	
Performance criteria	**Knowledge and understanding**
9.3 Use valid, fair, reliable and safe assessment methods	**KU10** How to make sure that assessment decisions are made against specified criteria and are valid, reliable and fair
9.4 Identify and collect evidence that is valid, authentic and sufficient	**KU11** How to determine when evidence is sufficient to make an assessment decision
9.5 Make assessment decisions against specified criteria	**KU12** How to judge the authenticity and currency of evidence and what to do when there is doubt

Assessor units	
Unit title	**Learning outcomes**
1 Understanding the principles and practices of assessment	**2** Understand different types of assessment methods **5** Understand how to make assessment decisions
2 Assess occupational competence in the work environment	**2** Be able to make assessment decisions about occupational competence
3 Assess vocational skills, knowledge and understanding	**2** Be able to carry out assessments of vocational skills, knowledge and understanding

Keeping it legal

You must ensure that your assessment practices and procedures comply with current legislation. The main laws that apply to you and your learners concern equality of opportunity on grounds of sex, race or disability, safeguarding and the use of information. These are:

- The Equality Act 2010

- The Safeguarding Vulnerable Groups Act 2006

- The Data Protection Act 1998.

This section describes the key points about the legislation you need to know about in your role as an assessor.

Discrimination

The Equality Act became law in October 2010, replacing the previous acts and regulations that formed the basis of anti-discrimination law in Great Britain. These included the Equal Pay Act 1970, the Sex Discrimination Act 1975, the Race Relations Act 1976, the Disability Discrimination Act 2005 and the Special Educational Needs and Disability Act 2001. It also replaces the three major statutory instruments protecting against discrimination in employment on grounds of religion or belief, sexual orientation and age.

This new legislation requires equal treatment in access to employment as well as private and public services, regardless of the 'protected characteristics' of age, disability, gender reassignment, marriage and civil partnership, race, religion or belief, sex, and sexual orientation. In the case of disability, employers and service providers are under a duty to make reasonable adjustments to their workplaces to overcome barriers experienced by disabled people. With limited exceptions the Act does not apply to Northern Ireland.

Legislation against discriminatory practice has come a long way since the 1970s, when it was introduced. It is no longer enough to say you have procedures in place; the general duty to promote equality is a positive one, requiring you and your organisation to be pro-active in seeking to avoid unlawful discrimination before it occurs.

Sex discrimination

When the Sex Discrimination Act 1975 was originally passed, it was designed to protect females, but now the laws apply to either sex. The legislation has also since been extended to offer transsexuals protection from discrimination on the grounds of gender in employment or vocational training.

'In care, we plan and assess holistically, which means we carry out assessment based on learner activities and their shifts and working patterns. If we didn't, we'd be indirectly discriminating against those with family responsibilities – often women.'

Key points

1 The Equality Act applies to all sex discrimination in the workplace, such as selection for a job, training, promotion, terms of employment, work practices, dismissal or any other disadvantage such as sexual harassment.

2 Responsibility for sex discrimination usually lies with the employer, but if an employee or worker is found to have discriminated, then the employer will be 'vicariously' liable for them as well. You or your organisation may not intend to discriminate, but this is not regarded as justification should you be taken to a tribunal.

3 Employers must act on any recommendations made by an employment tribunal, for the benefit of all employees, not just the claimant.

The law in Britain recognises two kinds of discrimination: direct and indirect.

Direct sex discrimination

This is where a person of one sex is treated less favourably on grounds of sex than someone of the other sex would have been treated in the same circumstances. An example might be using different terms and conditions for the same or similar standard of job.

Indirect sex discrimination

Indirect sex discrimination can occur where a requirement or condition is applied equally to men and women, but the proportion of one sex that can comply with the condition is much smaller than the proportion of the other sex. Unless it can be proven that the condition is essential for the job, indirect discrimination may have taken place. It has also been established that discrimination against part-time workers may constitute indirect discrimination against women because most part-time workers are women.

What this means in practice

When carrying out assessment, you need to ensure that the procedures and language you use are fair to both genders. This means:

- asking the same or similar questions of both males and females

- not favouring one gender over the other (overusing 'he' in your promotional literature, for example)

- checking that entry requirements (or those of the services you promote) do not require knowledge or experience that may disadvantage one gender over the other. For example, asking for experience of bringing up small children for a nursery nurse's position may put men at a disadvantage. Similarly, carrying out assessment only between the hours of 8:30am–5pm might disadvantage women with young children.

Racial discrimination

The law since 1975 has prohibited direct or indirect discrimination based on a person's race, which includes colour, nationality or ethnic origin. Since 2000 the law has gone even further, and requires organisations to promote racial equality and seek to avoid unlawful discrimination before it occurs.

The aim is to make race equality a central part of the way we all work, by putting it at the centre of policy-making, service delivery, regulation and enforcement, and employment practice. The laws protect everyone from racial discrimination at every stage of employment, including training (and, by implication, assessment). Since 2000 the law has also explicitly included all public authorities, and this may apply to you if your organisation is in receipt of government funding.

As with sex discrimination, you need to be aware of both direct and indirect discrimination.

Direct racial discrimination is where you treat someone less favourably because of his or her race, colour, nationality or ethnic origin.

Indirect racial discrimination could be where you use procedures or resources that may seem to apply to all, but actually discriminate against certain groups. This may happen in subtle ways. For example, giving out information only in English may be seen as indirect discrimination. Another example might be if your organisation insisted on a dress code that certain groups of women could not comply with for religious reasons.

What this means in practice

To ensure you comply with the law when assessing, you must:

- take account of cultural differences during face-to-face interviews (providing access to interpreters and using appropriate body language, for example)

- ensure that any assessment methods you use – such as self-assessments or tests – do not disadvantage one group over another because of the way they are used or scored

- ensure that the language you use is neutral and bias-free (avoiding colloquialisms or making assumptions that learners have local knowledge, for example).

Discrimination on grounds of disability

The law gives rights to those with disabilities in areas of employment and access to goods, services, facilities and buying or renting land or property.

Key points

1 The Act describes disability as follows:

   'a physical or mental impairment which has a substantial and long-term effect on a person's ability to carry out normal day-to-day activities. The disability is to have lasted or be likely to last 12 months or more. If a person has had a disability within this definition, they are protected from discrimination even if they are no longer disabled.'

2 Since 2010, to qualify for protection from discrimination, a disabled person no longer has to show that their impairment affects a particular 'capacity', such as mobility or speech, hearing or eyesight.

3 Under the Act, organisations have a duty to be anticipatory, that is, by making adjustments so that people with disabilities can access services where it is reasonable for the service provider to make these adjustments.

What this means in practice

To comply with the law when assessing, you must not:

- treat a disabled person less favourably because the person has a disability – this is 'direct discrimination'
- indirectly discriminate against a disabled person, unless there is a fair and balanced reason for this
- directly discriminate against or harass a person because they are associated with a disabled person, or wrongly thought to be disabled
- victimise anyone.

You may usually ask a person about their disability only to help you decide whether you need to adjust or adapt your assessment process. You have a duty to make reasonable changes to the way you assess, known as 'reasonable adjustments', to avoid putting a disabled learner at a disadvantage compared to a non-disabled learner. For example, you might need to provide special or adapted equipment or make physical adjustments to improve access (such as replacing steps with a ramp).

The quotations on the right are examples of anticipatory changes in practice.

'We introduced reading aloud to candidates with hearing impairments and found that other candidates preferred it, so now we offer it to everyone as part of our service.'

'We were considering providing assessment to learners with disabilities within their care settings. However, we realised that we would be denying them the benefits of group sessions and peer interaction, so we changed our offer.'

Centre manager

Safeguarding

The Safeguarding Vulnerable Groups Act 2006 applies to children and vulnerable adults. The definition of a vulnerable adult is quite wide, and includes anyone over 18 if they:

- are in residential accommodation or sheltered housing
- receive domiciliary care or any form of healthcare
- are detained in lawful custody
- are under the supervision of the courts
- receive welfare service of a prescribed description
- receive payments under the Health & Social Care Act 2001
- require assistance in the conduct of their own affairs.

The Act contains provision for the vetting and barring of individuals wishing to work with these groups, including specific requirements for them to register with the Independent Safeguarding Authority (ISA) and for Criminal Records Bureau (CRB) checks.

1 The Act defines two types of activity, regulated and controlled:

- **Regulated** activities are those frontline activities where people have frequent, direct contact with children or vulnerable adults in health, care or education.

- **Controlled** activities are those that fall outside regulated activities, but which involve contact with children or vulnerable adults and/or access to sensitive information concerning them.

2 It is a criminal offence for employers:

- to employ someone in either a controlled or a regulated activity if they fail to check the person's status.

- to allow a barred or unregistered person to work in a **regulated** activity.

3 Employees' responsibilities under the Act are as follows:

- A barred individual must not take part in any regulated activity.

- A person taking part in a regulated activity must be registered with the ISA.

- It is a criminal offence for an individual to take part in a regulated activity if they are barred.

4 A barred person can work in a controlled activity under certain circumstances, as long as safeguards are in place.

What this means in practice

The requirements of the Safeguarding Vulnerable Groups Act apply to you if you have frequent contact with children or vulnerable adults in your role as an assessor or teacher, such as those on apprenticeships, or prisoners.

Data protection

The Data Protection Act 1998 is the law that regulates processing and storage of personal information relating to individuals, including ways in which this information is used or disclosed. It covers all personal information, held electronically or otherwise.

Key points

1 Any organisations holding personal data electronically must register with the Data Protection Registrar, whose job is to enforce the Act.

2 When they register, organisations must specify the purpose for which they intend to use the data: this must be obtained lawfully and fairly.

3 Individuals have the right to know what information is held concerning them and to ask to see it.

4 If information is wrong, the organisation responsible must ensure that it is amended or deleted.

5 Information cannot be given to anyone (companies or individuals) who isn't entitled to it, and must be protected against unauthorised access, alteration, deletion or disclosure.

What this means in practice

All the information you obtain about your learners is covered by the Act, including information you may input electronically, such as:

- individual assessment and/or learning plans
- action plans
- application forms
- results of assessment
- emails containing personal information concerning specific learners.

To comply with the Act you need to do the following:

- Tell learners what personal information you need from them, and what will happen to it (who will see it and who won't, and how long you will keep it).
- Tell learners that they have a right to see whatever is written about them and that they can object to it if they want to. This means showing them what you have written about them after assessment.
- Advise learners that the centre, awarding organisation and/or qualifications regulator may need access to the information you hold on them.

Activity: Do we comply with the legislation?

Use your answers to the following questions to check that you comply with current legislation and identify areas for further action. Tick yes only if you have evidence that proves you do it in practice. Be strict with yourself here: if you don't know your organisation's policies or you haven't been trained in these areas, you are unlikely to be compliant should you or your organisation come under scrutiny.

Area of compliance	Yes, and we can prove it	Not sure	No
Do our assessment policies and procedures actively promote equality of opportunity for both sexes?	☐	☐	☐
Do we operate within the law on			
• direct sex discrimination?	☐	☐	☐
• indirect sex discrimination?	☐	☐	☐
Do our assessment policies and procedures show that we are proactive in promoting racial equality?	☐	☐	☐
Do we monitor the impact of our assessment policies and programmes to ensure that they are meeting the needs of ethnic minorities?	☐	☐	☐
Do we operate anticipatory procedures with regard to clients with disabilities?	☐	☐	☐
If applicable, are we working within the law with regard to children and/or vulnerable adults?	☐	☐	☐
Do we let learners know what information we hold on them and give them access to it if they request it?	☐	☐	☐

You are aiming to answer yes in all cases. Where you have answered no or not sure, you will have to take action to ensure that you comply with the law in these areas. Start by talking to your IQA and reading your organisational policies in each area of legislation.

What the standards say

National occupational standards (NOS) Standard 9: Assess learner achievement	
Knowledge and understanding	
KU9 Issues related to equality, diversity and, where relevant, bilingualism, that may affect the assessment process and how to address these	

Assessor units	
Unit title	**Learning outcomes**
1 Understanding the principles and practices of assessment	**8** Understand the legal and good practice requirements in relation to assessment
2 Assess occupational competence in the work environment	**4** Be able to maintain legal and good practice requirements when assessing occupational competence
3 Assess vocational skills, knowledge and understanding	**4** Be able to maintain legal and good practice requirements when assessing vocational skills, knowledge and understanding

Continuous professional development and reflective practice

Continuous professional development (CPD) is the process by which we keep up to date with current practice in our field, improve our skills, and progress into new roles. CPD helps us stay interested in our work, and motivated to take advantage of the many opportunities that come our way. With this in mind, you will need to keep up to date with the requirements for assessment practice, and you should also be prepared to undertake continuous professional development (CPD) activities so that your practice remains current against developments in the sector for which you are an assessor.

Reflection is an important part of CPD, since it will help you decide what your development needs are. This section will help you with the skills of critical reflection, using examples from other assessors. It tells you how to keep a reflective account, and how you can use it to enhance your skills when assessing.

Keeping a reflective account

As an assessor you need be able to reflect on your practice, so that you know whether or not you are effective. You must be able to reflect on what you do in terms of both maintaining the national standards and looking at your practice from your learners' point of view.

Being able to reflect critically on your own assessment practice means that you see for yourself where you may need to change the way you do things, or where you may need help. This ability will be of continuing benefit to your own practice and will also help improve the quality of assessment within your centre.

To know what your learning and development needs are, you need to be able to stand back from what you do in your day-to-day role. After each assessment episode, take time to reflect critically on what has gone well and what may have gone less well. Your IQA will help you with this when he or she observes you in action.

There are many ways of reflecting on your assessment practice; there are no hard and fast rules. Many assessors keep a reflective diary or an online log and make regular entries. It is especially helpful if you use it to focus on incidents that are significant to you and relevant to your practice.

Triggers for reflection to record might include:

- an article you have read on assessment, or a training course you attended

- an assessment episode that went badly

- one of your learners achieving success, or failing

- lack of support – or a welcome contribution – from a colleague or colleagues

- the introduction of a new way of assessing or of working.

Format and style

Most reflective accounts use a fairly informal, personal style (using 'I', 'we' or 'you'). Some people even use the 'Dear diary' format. You may find it helpful to use a list of questions to focus your thoughts, or other headings such a those used by the assessor who wrote the extract shown opposite. Using a series of questions or headings stops you getting stuck in describing the 'what happened and what do I feel about it?' stages and enables you to move on to reflecting on what you have learnt and what you will do next.

You may find that using the following checklist of questions is a helpful way of structuring your reflective account:

- *What happened?*

- *What went well and/or badly?*

- *How do I feel about this?*

- *What have I learnt?*

- *What will change as a result of what I have learnt?*

Read through the following extract from one assessor's reflective log. This was triggered following a training day she attended.

Key point

If your role also includes teaching and/or supporting learning – for example coaching in the workplace – and your organisation is in receipt of government funding, you will need to register with the Institute for Learning (IfL) for CPD purposes and gain an appropriate teaching qualification.

Reflective log
7 February 2011

Observation
(What happened?)

Today I attended a training session run by the ABC Awarding Organisation with one of my centre's IQAs.

In it we were told about holistic assessment, and experienced observation and discussion in action as well as using technology for capturing evidence. We also learned about ways of reducing bureaucracy when we record assessment decisions.

Reflection
(What went well/badly?
How do I feel about it?)

The course opened my eyes to what we should be doing as a centre and to how I should be assessing. I am surprised that I did not know about some of the approaches to assessment as I attend centre standardisation meetings and training days on a regular basis.

The course raised several issues for me personally and for the centre where I work:

1) I am not using observation of performance and discussion as the main ways of assessing learners in the work environment. As a centre, we give out pre-prepared portfolios to learners and get them to fill in the appropriate sections with paper-based evidence which we then go through with them and sign and date.

2) I didn't know that this practice was inappropriate until now.

3) How do I help other assessors? They need to realise that some of their practice is no longer appropriate.

4) How do I bring this to the centre manager's attention?

Remember

Triggers for reflection (sometimes called 'significant events') can be positive as well as negative. They can also be seemingly small incidents as well as large events or situations.

Review
(What have I learnt?)

I need to start putting some of the assessment methods I have learned about into practice with learners. However, I will need the backing of the centre manager to do so as we will need to change some of our approaches to assessment. I now find the practice of giving all learners a pre-prepared portfolio unacceptable as I realise this is putting the onus on the learner to find the evidence, whereas we were taught that as assessors we are in charge of the assessment process.

Action
(What will change?)

The situation has made me realise how important it is for senior managers to be on board with changes to assessment and quality assurance before they send front-line assessors and IQAs on training courses. As an approved centre we urgently need to update our practice if we are to provide high-quality assessment for our learners.

I will approach our centre manager and suggest that she meet the IQA and me, so that we can talk to her about the approaches we have learned with a view to cascading these to other members of staff.

What the standards say

National occupational standards (NOS) Standard 9: Assess learner achievement		
Knowledge and understanding		
KU18 The value and purpose of continuing professional development for assessment practitioners		

Assessor units		
Unit title	**Learning outcomes**	**Assessment criteria**
1 Understanding the principles and practices of assessment	**8** Understand the legal and good practice requirements in relation to assessment	**8.4** Explain the value of reflective practice and continuing professional development in the assessment process
2 Assess occupational competence in the work environment	**4** Be able to maintain legal and good practice requirements when assessing occupational competence	**4.3** Evaluate own work in carrying out assessments of occupational competence
		4.4 Maintain the currency of own expertise and competence as relevant to own role in assessing occupational competence

Part 2
The assessment methods toolkit

Good assessment always means using a variety of methods for evaluating a learner's competence. This section of the guide describes in more detail the different assessment methods, what they involve and how and when to use them. The methods are:

- observation of performance

- examining work products and questioning

- discussion

- using others and learner statements

- using projects, assignments and case studies

- using simulated environments

- skills tests

- recognising prior learning (RPL).

Activity: *How well do I know the assessment methods?*

To help you get the most from the toolkit, answer the following questions
honestly in relation to each of the main assessment methods.

Questions	Yes	No	Not sure	Turn to pages
Observation of performance				
• Do you know what observation involves?	☐	☐	☐	55–6
• Are you 100 per cent confident about using it?	☐	☐	☐	56–7
• Can you record the results effectively?	☐	☐	☐	57–60
Examining work products and questioning				
• Are you confident about using evidence the learner has produced as a result of their work?	☐	☐	☐	62–3
• Do you know how to use work products with other suitable assessment methods?	☐	☐	☐	62
• Do you know how to use effective oral questioning with work products?	☐	☐	☐	63–6
Discussion				
• Have you been trained in how to use discussion with learners?	☐	☐	☐	67–8
• Do your learners understand their role in discussion?	☐	☐	☐	68–9
• Do you and your learners know what to do before, during and after a discussion?	☐	☐	☐	69–72
Using others and learner statements				
Do you know…				
• when to use contributions from other people?	☐	☐	☐	74
• how to identify suitable people?	☐	☐	☐	75
• how to brief others?	☐	☐	☐	76
• the best ways to capture others' accounts?	☐	☐	☐	76–8
• what a good written contribution from another person looks like (or sounds like if it's recorded)?	☐	☐	☐	77
• when to use learner statements?	☐	☐	☐	78
Projects, assignments and case studies				
Do you know when to use these methods?	☐	☐	☐	82–3
Do you know how to assess them?	☐	☐	☐	84–5
Simulation, skills testing and written questions				
Are you confident about using the following, where appropriate:				
• simulation?	☐	☐	☐	90–91
• skills testing?	☐	☐	☐	92–4
• written questions?	☐	☐	☐	94
Recognition of prior learning (RPL)				
Do you know what RPL is?	☐	☐	☐	95
Do you know the process of RPL?	☐	☐	☐	96–7

If you have answered no or not sure to any of the questions, turn to the
relevant section(s) first.

Observation
of performance

If the standards you assess are about performing under real-life working conditions, the best way to assess learners is by seeing them in action in the workplace. This is why most assessment strategies tell you to use observation of performance as your main method of assessment. A major part of your job is therefore to watch learners demonstrate their practical skills as they go about their job activities in their work environment.

Observation is the obvious form of workplace assessment: you watch someone doing something to see if they can do it properly. It is also the most valid and reliable assessment method, because you can be sure that the evidence you see is both authentic and up to date. Using observation also makes assessment relevant and meaningful for the learner because it takes place in the context of their normal work.

However, it is important to develop some rules for observation, so that everyone involved in the process understands clearly what is being looked for, and what evidence is required to determine whether or not the standards have been met. It also helps to know thoroughly both the standards for which you are assessing and the job you are assessing. (This is why assessment strategies specify the amount and type of experience expected of assessors.)

This chapter explains the key considerations for using observation, how to plan and carry out observation sessions, and how to record your assessment decisions.

Key considerations for using observation

Generally, you're aiming to observe the learner carrying out the main tasks they do as part of their job. Your starting point is the assessment strategy and evidence requirements for the qualification: these specify what must be observed and state how many times this must be seen.

To use observation successfully, however, you need to know how to make the most of it. On its own, observation doesn't tell you enough about how the learner performs over time and across a range of conditions, and you're unlikely to cover all the knowledge and understanding, even if you use clever questioning. This means that you have to use observation in combination with other assessment methods. For example, other people's accounts can tell you about the learner's performance over time, and product evidence (things the learner has produced as a result of their work) could also support what you have seen.

How to carry out observation

Use the following steps when planning and carrying out observation.

1 **Before the observation**

As with all assessment strategies, the key to effective observation is good planning. You will need to work with your learner in advance of the observation to set a date and time, plan in outline what you want to observe, and tell them whether and when you will ask them questions during the observation. You will need to be prepared to be flexible, however, since what actually happens will depend on what the learner faces at work on the day. You also need to plan around the whole activity, and include evidence that will become available after the observation, so that the learner can arrange for you to have access to this.

2 **During the observation**

Before you start, try to put the learner at ease, so that they will be able to carry out their activities as they normally would. It helps to go through again what you'll be doing, reminding them about what you planned together. Tell them that you may take notes from time to time during the observation, but that these will be for your own benefit as reminders rather than comments on performance.

Make a note of anything you want to follow up. For example, you might want to ask them why they carried out a task in a particular order.

Choose a suitable point at which to question the learner, having discussed this with them at the planning stage. If they're moving around or tackling a variety of tasks, it may make sense to question them as you go along, otherwise they could forget what they were doing and why they were doing it.

3 **After the observation**

Ask any supplementary questions you have at this stage. Even these may not provide you with the full picture, however: the learner may have to provide more evidence, and you may need to go and see it if it's available.

'We're in an old Victorian signal box at 8:30am and I'm meant to be observing my learner, a signalman. He arrives late, so we've got 45 minutes to wait before I can observe him deal with the next train. You think: what can I do? You start a conversation and ask him about his job. You're thinking: "Knowledge and understanding: let's see his paperwork, then ask him some questions about procedures." Now he's digging out his health and safety policies and I'm asking him questions about how they apply.'

Give the learner feedback on how well they've done:

- Tell them which of the assessment criteria they have met.
- Explain which of the assessment criteria they haven't met, and why.
- Be specific about what happens next. You may need to go back to your original assessment plan and say, for example: 'I've seen you give a presentation to a group of eight, and now we have to verify your performance with other groups. For this we need a statement from your training manager.' (This should already be part of the overall assessment plan, but you may need to contact the learner's manager at this point.)

Gathering evidence through observation

Using observation as an assessment method should give you enough evidence about an aspect of a learner's performance to be able to make a judgement about their competence against the standards, but it can sometimes be difficult to know when you've seen enough evidence. If you've agreed a half-day session for observation, for example, you may feel obliged to stay until the end of the agreed time even though you have seen enough before then. The standards should always be your main guide.

Activity: Have I seen enough evidence?

This checklist will help you decide when you've gained enough evidence.

Have I seen evidence that ...	Yes	No
• all the relevant learning outcomes and assessment criteria have been covered?	☐	☐
• all likely performance conditions have been covered?	☐	☐
• the underpinning knowledge and understanding have been covered (by questioning or other methods)?	☐	☐
• that this person performs consistently to the standards?	☐	☐

You are aiming to answer yes in each case. If you answer no, you may need to observe again, or use other methods to assess further evidence.

Recording observation evidence

It's not enough simply to make an assessment decision as a result of your observation. You have to be able to explain how and why you arrived at your decision, so that you can give useful feedback to the learner on their performance, and for quality purposes. This is why the IQA quoted on this page took issue with the assessor: it wasn't that the assessor didn't know what he was observing, it's that he didn't explain how he arrived at his decision or use the evidence he saw to back it up.

The following report, showing how one assessor recorded her assessment of a learner assessor in an estate agency through observation and other methods, is an example of good practice. The report records the methods used to assess the activities, the units and assessment criteria covered, the location of evidence and her assessment decision. The report also links to the assessment plan on page 28, and shows you how the assessor records her observations and assessment decisions based on the plan.

'I came across an example of assessment by observation where the assessor simply stated that he "observed the learner take on duties" with no further detail or evidence. He then made the decision that the learner was competent. As his IQA, I couldn't agree with his decision.'

Assessment report

Learner	Qualification
Stephen Jackson	L3 Certificate in assessing vocational achievement

Date of assessment	Location of assessment
23 and 26 June 2011	Peters and Wright Estate Agents

Assessor	Units assessed
Ameera Patel	Units 1, 2 & 3 (incomplete)

Date, assessment activities and assessment methods used	Unit and assessment criteria	Location of evidence
23 JUNE 2011: OBSERVATION I observed Stephen observing his learner Keira working with a client in the office. (Keira is working towards her NVQ3 in customer service.) Stephen met with Keira before the assessment and confirmed Keira's understanding of the planned assessment activity with her. It was clear from the discussion with his learner that Stephen had involved Keira in the planning process, and that Keira was prepared for the assessment. The timing of the assessment had been set at a time and place that met both Keira's and her employers' needs, and was based around the activities that she was carrying out as part of her working day.	Unit 1 4.2, 4.4, 3.1, 3.3, 3.5	Observation report in learner's file (kept in the centre filing cabinet)
Stephen observed Keira as she greeted clients; assessed their needs; completed company documentation; and added details to the client database. Stephen recorded appropriately a verbal account from the client during the process, to confirm that Keira had met the necessary NVQ standards in relation to customer satisfaction. Stephen examined products from performance (client history and details). He then asked Keira questions that confirmed her underpinning knowledge with regard to the work she had carried out. Stephen made his assessment decision and filled in the documentation appropriately.	Unit 2 1.1, 1.2, 1.3, 1.4, 2.1	Client database, Peters and Wright Estate Agents, Holloway Road RG10 9TQ
I observed Stephen giving feedback to Keira. This was done during Keira's tea break. He gave her feedback on the assignment she had completed, including his assessment decision. The feedback was given in private. Stephen began by asking Keira to assess her own performance. He then explained the assessment decision by explaining the areas where Keira had demonstrated her competence. He then produced the next assessment plan with Keira. This was based around a survey to enable Keira to evaluate the effectiveness of the service her office provides. They agreed areas for further development and how these would be met during her off-job training.	Unit 2 2.2, 3.1, 4.1, 4.2, 2.4	Assessment documentation in learner's file

EXAMINING WORK PRODUCTS I examined the completed assessment plan, assessment record, decision and judgment. All evidence had been captured and referenced against the standards met. The location of the evidence was clearly indicated. All were completed on time and in line with centre requirements.	Unit 3 1.1, 2.1, 2.2, 2.3, 2.4, 2.6	
26 JUNE 2011: QUESTIONING AND DISCUSSION I carried out a discussion and questioning of Stephen via Skype. This was digitally recorded, and can be found in Sound File 3. During the discussion Stephen confirmed the process by which he had planned, set, assessed and judged the assignment that formed part of this assessment. 1 MIN 20 SECS Stephen explained the functions of assessment (of learning and for learning) in learning and development, the responsibilities of learner, assessor and internal quality assurer. 6 MINS 30 SECS	Unit 2 2.3 3.1, 3.2, 3.3 4.1, 4.2	Sound File 3: Learner file
Stephen explained the reasons behind his choice of assessment methods, and how he combined them to assess a number of units holistically on this assessment occasion. He explained how this benefited the learner and how he safeguarded the process to ensure reliability. 11 MINS 20 SECS Stephen described occasions when he would use particular assessment methods and others when he would not use certain assessment methods. He also described how basing assessment on the learner's real work enabled him to involve them in the process. 15 MINS 25 SECS	Unit 1 1.1–1.4, 1.1–1.2, 3.1–3.5 4.1–4.4, 2.1	
Stephen described how he arrived at his assessment decision and the processes he uses to ensure that he obtains safe, authentic, valid evidence and makes fair and reliable decisions. 17 MINS 10 SECS The full discussion providing evidence of knowledge can be found on the sound file. The above assessment activities and evidence confirm competence in the units and assessment criteria recorded here. *Ameera Patel* 26 June 2011	5.1, 5.2	

Here are some do's and don'ts to bear in mind when using observation.

Do	Don't
• think in terms of producing written records. These are more powerful for observations, as you can use them more than once to cover other standards.	• rely solely on one observation as proof of the learner's ability to perform consistently and under different conditions. Back it up where necessary by using discussion and/or questioning to capture any knowledge that is inferred through performance.
• think in terms of producing a 'narrative' which describes the main points of what you see when recording your observations. (See the assessor's report on the previous two pages for a good example of this.)	• assess without first planning what you are going to assess, and agreeing it with the learner (but take account of any naturally occurring evidence as it happens)
• ensure that all relevant people, such as the learner and his or her employer, know that the observation is taking place.	• fill in pre-prepared checklists – they can be limiting. Use the standards as your main reference point instead.
• agree the best time for observations to take place with your learner, and be prepared to involve their employer or manager if you plan to observe them at a busy time, or when carrying out a sensitive task.	

Activity: Am I ready to carry out an observation?

Successful observation practice depends on the following factors.
Tick the ones that apply to you. You are aiming for a row of ticks before you begin your observation:

Factor	Tick
1 Am I familiar with the assessment strategy and evidence requirements for the qualification?	☐
2 Do I know the standards I am assessing, and where they occur in the activities I am about to observe?	☐
3 Do I know about the learner's job and/or their occupation?	☐
4 Have I made sure that the learner, the employer and any others (such as the learner's line manager) know about what's involved in the observation process?	☐
5 Do I have the information I need about the workplace and the learner's job role?	☐
6 Do I have the permission or support of the person in charge to go in and observe?	☐
7 Does the learner know what I will be observing, and why?	☐

Examining work
products and questioning

Work products arise naturally as a result of what learners do. A work product is anything the learner produces as a result of their work, and might be a care plan, a brick wall or a haircut; or a successful outcome such as a report or an interaction with a client. You will see learners producing work products when you are observing them, and once you have seen your learner in action you will want to follow up what you have seen by using questioning.

Asking the learner questions follows naturally from looking at their work products, and is one of the main methods to use to find out whether or not your learner has the necessary knowledge and understanding of the tasks they are performing.

This chapter tells you:

- how work products and questioning work together

- how to use work products as evidence

- how and when to use questioning, and which questioning techniques to use

- how to record and assess the evidence from work products and questioning.

How work products and questioning work together

You need to know what your learner is likely to produce by way of work products, so that you can include these at the planning stage, along with the assessment methods you will use. The following diagram shows what it might look like in practice when you are assessing a learner assessor's competence in assessment planning:

Activity: Choosing the right assessment method

Which assessment methods would you use for items 1–3 if you were the assessor for the following example? And which one is the work product you would need to examine? (Answers at the bottom of page 63)

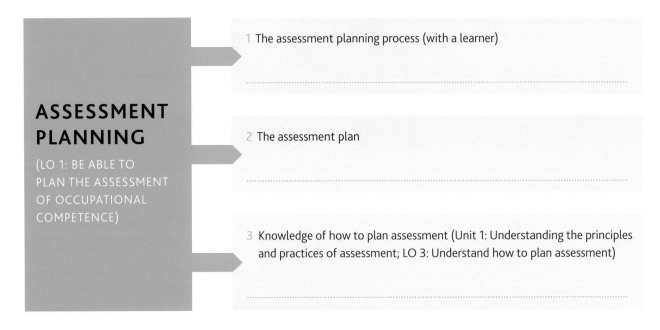

ASSESSMENT PLANNING

(LO 1: BE ABLE TO PLAN THE ASSESSMENT OF OCCUPATIONAL COMPETENCE)

1 The assessment planning process (with a learner)

2 The assessment plan

3 Knowledge of how to plan assessment (Unit 1: Understanding the principles and practices of assessment; LO 3: Understand how to plan assessment)

Examining work products

Examining work products isn't strictly an assessment method, because you're looking at the outcomes or end product of learners' performance (as opposed to, or in addition to, watching them actually perform). However, examining work products is an important part of your job as an assessor, helping you to build up a picture of the learner's overall competence because you can't always be there to observe a learner in action.

Examples of work products are:

- invoices
- plans
- reports
- budgets
- items that the learner has made (recorded in photographs or videos if the item is big)

In some cases the products of learners' work are concrete (a report, a decorated room, a tiled roof, a door that's been hung or a plumbed-in central heating system). In other cases the outcomes aren't as obvious (a satisfied customer, a nutritious meal), or may only happen occasionally (a stock take, or changing suppliers).

Recording and assessing the evidence

When assessing work products, bear in mind that, on their own, products aren't evidence of competence. You need to assess them using the other main assessment methods and record these in the normal way, for example:

- observing the learner producing them

- using another person's account of how they were produced or how they meet the standards

- asking how and why they were produced, as part of a discussion

- using questioning to establish the learner's underpinning knowledge of how and why the products were produced.

All the products that the learner shows you *must* be the result of the work they carry out. You should not set learners an assignment on something they already cover in their normal work, as this places an unnecessary burden on them.

Learners don't have to provide you with new or different products for every unit in the standards. Work products can be used more than once to cover several elements or units, provided you think they are relevant and they meet the VAS criteria when you're assessing them.

How to use questioning

When questioning, you may need to find out more about the learner's implicit performance. This may be something you have not seen in action but which is an obvious part of the task or job. You may also want to question the learner about other aspects of their job that are related to the standards, such as what they might do under different circumstances or conditions.

Questioning goes hand in hand with examining work products and observation, and is also an integral part of discussion and using another person's account of the learner's knowledge and performance. You also use questioning to establish a learner's knowledge and understanding, and to fill gaps in your knowledge of their competence, in addition to using other assessment methods.

Oral questioning is obviously the best method to use. Only give learners prepared questions in cases where you know the evidence is necessary, and if you won't see them face to face. Don't use prepared lists of questions that are given out to all learners irrespective of their circumstances. See page 94 for more about using written questions.

Asking questions effectively

Asking the right questions is at the heart of effective communication and of gaining the information you need. For assessment you can use various types of question in different ways, depending on the type of information you need from your learner. Common questioning techniques include using:

- open questions

- closed questions

- probing questions

- hypothetical (what if?) questions.

Key points

To count as valid evidence, work products need to:

- show how the learning outcomes and assessment criteria apply in a working context

- concern real work in real time carried out by the learner

- be instigated by the organisation, or be of direct benefit to it.

Learners need to be able to explain how their work products meet the relevant standards. This is where you can use questioning or discussion as additional assessment methods.

Activity answers

You will probably have said:

- You would use observation for No. 1: The assessment planning process with a learner.

- You would use questioning for No. 3: Knowledge of how to plan assessment.

- The work product you would need to examine is No. 2: The assessment plan.

Open questions

Open questions usually include the words:

why	*what*
where	*how*
who	*when*

You use open questions when you want more than a one-word answer. Use them, for example, when you want to encourage learners to give a detailed explanation of something you have observed them doing, or to tell you how they produced the work product you are examining.

Closed questions

Closed questions require a short or one-word answer such as 'Yes', 'No' or 'The red fire extinguisher'. Using closed questions can help you:

- check key knowledge – for example, 'Would you use the red fire extinguisher if there had been an electrical fault?'

- check your own understanding – for example, 'Are you saying you would use the green fire extinguisher?'

Probing questions

Probing questions are follow-up questions, to ask when you want to find out more. Probing is more than a request for further information; you are aiming to go deeper into what the learner knows and to find out whether they know the reasons why they have performed in certain ways. You will find it useful to probe if the standards require you to assess higher-order cognitive skills such as learners' abilities to analyse and evaluate.

Repeating back the learner's exact words is a simple way of asking a probing question, for example, 'You say you used the company procedure for dealing with the complaint; what did that involve exactly?'

Probing questions are useful when you want to get beyond any superficial or rehearsed answers to questions. You can also use them in order to clarify any inconsistencies in a learner's answers.

Hypothetical questions and case studies

Hypothetical questions use or imply the words 'What if?'

Here is an example of how one assessor uses a case study for asking hypothetical questions in relation to using company procedures for discriminatory practice:

'Your supervisor informs you that one of your operatives is being racially harassed by other workers. The employee in question has been taking increasing amounts of time off work as sick leave.

1 What procedures are there for your workforce to report problems, either work-related or personal?

2 How would you deal with this particular situation?'

You can also use such questions to establish your learner's knowledge of how to cope with contingencies, rare and unusual occurrences, or emergency situations.

'I'm assessing in the care home, and I see the learner closing the door after he enters the client's room. Later on, I make a point of asking him, "Why did you close the door?" "Because I've seen all the others do it", was his answer. He had no concept of maintaining clients' dignity or privacy.'

Remember

When using questioning to find out more about something, keep asking supplementary questions, focusing on the points the learner raises, until you get to the detail you require.

Tip

Use questions that include the word 'exactly' to probe further: 'What exactly do you mean by estimate?'; 'Who, exactly, wanted this report?'

Leading questions

Leading questions are phrased in such a way that the answer is obvious, for example:

'You aren't telling me you would use water to extinguish an electrical fire, are you?'

As an assessor, you should avoid leading questions because they reveal nothing about the learner and can give you a false impression of their abilities. Even experienced assessors describe using leading questions without meaning to when they arrive at a premature decision about the learner's achievement. They find themselves asking the kind of question that can only confirm their decision, such as 'So, are you happy that you can carry out the job like that again?' without probing more deeply.

Using the right question at the right time

It is important to develop the ability to choose the most appropriate type of question in a given context. This will enable your learner to demonstrate what they know because they have already been in that situation, rather than asking them to imagine their response to a hypothetical scenario. The quotation on the right gives an example of this.

Remember

Hypothetical questions and case studies ask learners to *imagine* how they might behave in a particular scenario or situation, and are appropriate for assessing knowledge-based learning outcomes and/or assessment criteria. If the standards require them actually to perform, you should be observing them first and asking this type of question afterwards, to supplement and extend what you have seen. This applies particularly to complex scenarios or situations.

See pages 81–8 for more about projects, assignments and case studies.

'Assessment criteria in our Level 2 award concern emergency procedures and ask the learner to demonstrate that they know and understand "offering comfort and reassurance" or "how to raise the alarm". Assessors often used stock "what if" questions when the learner has actually dealt with an incident. The questions they should be using are "Have you ever had to comfort an injured person? What did you do?", or "Have you ever had to raise the alarm in an emergency situation? What did you do?", or "Show me how you would..."'

Internal quality assurer

Recording and assessing the evidence

Learners will refer to all kinds of potential evidence during the course of questioning. Your job is to show how their answers form meaningful evidence of performance or knowledge, and to capture this when you're reaching and recording your assessment decisions.

For example, if the learner refers to relevant company procedures during questioning, ask questions about how they are used, and then ask to see the procedures. Record the fact that you have seen them and where they are kept, as part of your assessment decision against the relevant standards.

See the example on pages 58–9 for how you might record this.

Key points

- Question learners only on what is required in the standards, and nothing more.

- Try to link your questions directly to what the learner does in their workplace.

- Don't ask leading questions, or you will find yourself making the wrong assumptions (or judging your own competence and not the learner's).

Discussion

Discussion is another essential assessment method. It allows you to take a holistic approach to assessing a wide range of standards, and is the main method to use when you're assessing complex tasks and the learner's ability to show and apply in-depth knowledge.

Learners usually like using discussion, as it allows them to take the lead in demonstrating their learning in detail. It also enables them to discuss why and how something is done, and to fill in any gaps in their existing performance and knowledge evidence. Experienced assessors also like it, as it is one of the best ways to test the validity and reliability of the learner's evidence, particularly if they have used a range of activities covering a number of units. As assessment methods, discussion and questioning overlap: you are bound to ask questions during a discussion, but you are expecting your learner to lead the process more, having prepared for the discussion in advance.

This chapter will help you plan, conduct and capture the results of discussions with your learners. It covers:

- the key principles of discussion

- when to use discussion with your learners

- how to prepare for a discussion

- the five steps to follow during a discussion

- how to give meaningful feedback to the learner

- recording discussion outcomes.

Key considerations for using discussion

The principles of professional discussion are that:

- it works best when the learner is well prepared and able to participate

- it does not replace observation; the learner must still undertake and achieve all the practical activities defined in the units

- it needs to be recorded, either electronically or in note form.

The discussion should be an in-depth, two-way conversation between the assessor and the learner, which will enable you to gain a rounded picture of your learner's total performance. When used correctly, discussion avoids the need for large portfolios and bureaucracy, as you can simply talk to your learner about their performance and the reasons behind their actions and decisions.

There are no hard and fast rules for conducting discussions: much depends on how you respond to what your learner says and on your skill in moving the discussion forward if necessary. However, such discussions work best when you both know what you will be discussing, and when the learner has had enough time to prepare and so feels relaxed about talking to you.

Here is a summary of what professional discussion is and isn't about:

Remember

You wouldn't normally use discussions in isolation – they need to be backed up with appropriate evidence of work products or observations of the learner in action.

Discussion is about ...	Discussion is not about ...
• planning with your learner in advance the areas of the standards that will be under discussion and allowing your learner to prepare for the discussion.	• using a predetermined list of questions in a structured or mechanistic way.
• talking with the learner about what he or she is doing and the reasons why; you are looking for evidence of decision-making and analytical abilities as well as proof of specific knowledge.	• having a friendly chat.
• a gradual 'handing over' to the learner: after the initial discussion you would expect him or her to be taking the lead in any further discussion session.	• written case studies, storyboards or photocopies of evidence.
• recording the main points of what the learner says and how this relates to the relevant standards (using a bullet list, for example, supported by a recording of the discussion).	• recording verbatim what your learner says.
• you acquiring skills in:	• you telling your learner what to do.
◦ interviewing, listening and questioning	
◦ using video, audio or computer equipment (discussions can be taped or streamed as long as you check first that the learner is comfortable with this)	
◦ managing the discussion process (moving your learner on, and using summarising, questioning and clarifying techniques, for example)	
◦ picking out the key elements from the standards for which you are assessing, and concentrating on these.	

When to use discussion

Discussion is an ideal method to use when assessing for higher-level qualifications, where you would expect learners to present their own evidence. In some instances, where two or more learners may have similar evidence or where it is not immediately apparent how the evidence relates to the learner, use discussion of the evidence to clarify this.

In some industries where it is a statutory requirement to achieve a specific qualification – as in the waste industry – there are potential issues with regard to the copying of evidence. There was an instance where an external verifier spotted two identical portfolios that had been submitted through different assessors and different centres.

Some assessors use discussion in place of questioning, or to follow up on a written reflective account (see page 79). The value of a discussion over questioning is that it gives the learner an opportunity to offer evidence that might not always be easy to identify in a short question-and-answer session. A discussion is something that can develop naturally, allowing the learner to show qualities and characteristics that might otherwise be missed, and to explore underlying issues such as how the learner went about tackling a particular task, what they learned from the activity, and why they followed a particular course of action. This helps to integrate assessment.

Discussion is also an important part of assessing learners with particular needs, such as dyslexia, since it allows them to show their knowledge of the subject area in a way that best suits them. Discussion is also appropriate when the learner needs to talk about sensitive or confidential issues.

'I use discussion to check authenticity and clarify relevance. This is important in my industry as there are statutory requirements to achieve specific qualifications, so there are instances where learners may have similar evidence.'

Planning discussions

The key to carrying out a successful discussion is careful planning. As with any form of assessment, this requires time and effort from both you and your learner. You will need your learner to agree to the plan, and understand when the discussion will take place and how long it will last. They need to be happy with the timing of it, know what they want to achieve from it, and know what will happen afterwards. The discussion will not be useful unless both you and your learner are well prepared: you both need to know in advance what he or she will be talking about, and you will need to identify what, if anything, they need to bring with them.

Areas the learner may need to prepare for include:

- any specific knowledge they need to cover, and how they might do this. For example, if you are assessing cognitive skills such as their ability to evaluate, they may need to explain the advantages and disadvantages behind different courses of action, then choose one and explain it to you

- work products they may need to show you, and the reasons why they are doing so

- any complex tasks or procedures they need to talk about.

Many assessors find that they need to set aside at least an hour for discussion. This needs to be recorded on the assessment plan, which should reference all the standards to be assessed.

'Even though we had evidence already recorded in the portfolio and elsewhere, discussion with my dyslexic learner was a great way of combining the knowledge evidence with evidence of practical ability, and we both felt it strengthened the assessment process.'

In advance of the session, it's a good idea to give a copy of the assessment plan to the learner and any others who may be involved, such as the learner's trainer or line manager.

Activity: Preparing for discussion

Use the following checklist to help you identify what needs to be done with your learner at the planning stage. You are both aiming for a row of ticks.

Assessor		Learner	
1 Have I checked the units/learning outcomes and assessment strategy, to ensure that: • everything is covered? • discussion is the appropriate method to use?	☐	1 Do I know the topics I will be expected to discuss, and how these relate to the standards?	☐
2 Am I sure that this learner is ready to be assessed?	☐	2 Do I know what products or examples of my work I need to bring with me to the discussion?	☐
3 Have I decided how this discussion will be used in combination with other assessment methods (like observation and examining work products)?	☐	3 Do I have I enough time to prepare?	☐
4 Have I explained to the learner that I'll be listening for their real experience in the workplace?	☐	4 Am I confident about taking part in a discussion?	☐
5 Have we agreed a time and place to meet?	☐	5 Have we agreed a time and place to meet?	☐

Carrying out discussion

Follow these five steps during a discussion.

1 Put your learner at ease

It's easy to forget that some of your learners may find the prospect of a discussion an alarming one. A learner may be very good at their job but not confident about talking to an assessor. Since it's important that your learner feels relaxed during the discussion, and not that it's an ordeal to get through, it's a good idea to build in to your practice ways of reducing the learner's anxiety as much as possible. It helps to include an introduction to every discussion, when you outline what your learner should expect to happen during the conversation. One way of doing this is to lay some ground rules before you start (see note 2).

2 Lay ground rules and explain them before you start

For example, you could tell the learner that:

* they may ask questions

* they may take notes, or make their own recording of the conversation

* it's important that they talk about their own experience, and apply the theory to their own real practice

* you will stop them and move them on to the next topic when you have heard enough.

3 Encourage, focus and move on

Your job is to keep up the pace of the discussion and to steer it where necessary. This means:

- encouraging your learner to keep talking when they're on the right track, using active listening skills such as nodding, or saying, 'Tell me more…'

- keeping them focused on the standards and learning outcomes in question

- moving them on when they've covered the topic in enough depth. Use specific statements and questions such as, 'I'd like you to talk about the main methods of assessment you used. Why did you choose them?' Don't be afraid to interrupt if they wander off the point. Say something like, 'Can I interrupt you?' and follow it with a specific prompt question. (See Questioning on pages 63–5 for more on this.)

4 Identify further opportunities

Listen for anything your learner says that may provide further evidence of their performance, and ask to see it, or talk later to those involved, for their account of what your learner can do (using others; see below and pages 73–80).

5 Bring the discussion to a close

Give a clear signal that the discussion is at an end, by saying something like, 'That's great. I think we can end it there.'

Giving feedback

When you've finished, your learner will want to know how well they've done, and it's your job to tell them. When you do this, follow the general principles for giving feedback (see page 34). Immediately after a discussion, you may both want to take a break, particularly if you've been in a long conversation. This is definitely advisable if you're new to assessing, as it allows you to gather your thoughts before making your final decisions, and to be clear about what that the learner needs to do next.

Next steps

Agree on what the learner has to do next. For example, they may need to provide further evidence, particularly if you've identified new sources or they haven't met all the standards in question. Be specific about what they need to bring or do in relation to the standards.

If you think the learner's evidence needs further corroboration, you may need to identify and arrange to speak to other people who can tell you about their knowledge or performance, or arrange to observe the learner.

Record these next steps as action points and agree them with the learner, along with timescales.

'I had one learner who was highly nervous, and the thought of a discussion with me was giving her sleepless nights. I checked with the awarding body that it was okay to get her manager to carry out the discussion as part of her annual appraisal, which then formed a "using others" record which I followed up with questioning.'

Recording discussion outcomes

It is up to you how you structure or record the outcomes of a discussion. There are several possible ways to do it, but your guiding principles should always be to:

- approach it in a holistic way, that is, allowing the discussion to unfold naturally first, then making links to the standards when you make your assessment decision rather than going through the standards sequentially

- keep your record precise, clear and objective

- include your assessment decision linked to the learner's evidence, by referring to the digital recording, or the point during the discussion where the learner met the standard in question.

The example on pages 58–9 shows one possible way of recording the results of a discussion following observation of performance.

The blank page approach

Experienced assessors often choose the 'blank page' approach when recording the results of discussion. This means recording what the learner says as they go along, rather than taking a straight-line approach through the standards. This method assumes an in-depth knowledge of both the learning outcomes and assessment criteria and how they are assessed, so you need to be confident about your knowledge of these before using it.

Using others
and learner statements

Using others is where you identify a suitable person who can tell you what your learner knows and can do (this used to be known as a 'witness testimony'). Since you can't be there all the time to observe your learner in action at work, you can make use of other people's accounts of what the learner can do. A good witness can tell you a lot about how a learner performs over a period of time and under different conditions. They can say what they know about the learner, and describe activities or tasks the learner has carried out that relate to the standards in question.

Statements from learners can take the form of a reflective account or a written (b)log by the learner themselves, describing something they have done and reflecting on the outcomes. Because they are a form of self-reporting, for assessment purposes, these are not the same as statements from other people as they are not an objective account from a third party. However, they are a useful way of supplementing other forms of assessment.

This chapter has information on:

- when to use others' accounts

- how to identify and brief them

- the different ways of recording their account so that it constitutes valid evidence.

You will also find an example of a learner statement and suggestions about how and when to use such statements.

When to use others

Your own observation will yield only a snapshot of how a learner performs on the day you visit; an appropriate other person is someone who can tell you about other occasions when the learner has carried out the activity you've observed. Another person's account is also useful when the outcomes of a learner's work are brief or transitory, and it's difficult for you to be in the right place at the right time to see them perform. Reliable accounts from other people will confirm whether the learner:

- **performs consistently when carrying out important routine procedures**
  (for example, disposing of waste correctly; making good use of resources; following health and safety procedures at all times; or maintaining clients' dignity as a matter of routine)

- **deals with a one-off occurrence competently**
  (for example, an emergency; a customer problem; or an annual stock-take)

- **performs in situations where confidentiality or sensitivity is an issue**
  (for example, giving confidential advice and guidance; bathing an elderly service user in a care home; or giving someone a massage at a health spa).

You need to be specific about what the person needs to contribute. This might be:

- a written description of occasions when they have seen the learner perform to the standards in question, and the conditions under which they performed

- notes added to a project or assignment that the learner has carried out, and/or speaking to you, the assessor, about these.

As part of my observation of the learner, I get permission to question one of the hotel guests, then ask them how well they thought the receptionist dealt with them.'

Who can be a witness?

Other people acting as witnesses can be drawn from both the working and vocational environments. They can include supervisors, line managers and experienced colleagues from inside the learner's organisation, or from other organisations such as customers or clients. They may may also be a tutor or trainer. The person who regularly supervises a learner's performance in the working environment is often in the best position to say whether or not the learner is performing consistently to the standards over time. Using this person's contribution confirms to you that the learner is competent in a particular area.

Ensuring reliability

To ensure that the person you are using is reliable, it makes sense to find out about their experience and competence. Some assessment strategies clearly state who can and can't act in this capacity. This may mean asking the person to give details of their experience and/or qualifications.

The person you use is not expected to be an expert in assessment or the standards, but should be someone who can provide a written statement about the quality of a learner's work for assessment purposes, and who can declare first-hand experience of their performance and understanding. You can use other learners if, for example, they observed your learner dealing with an emergency or conflict situation. However, you need to be sure that their accounts are reliable and authentic.

Ultimately, you have to decide in each case whether or not the person can provide a valid statement about a learner's performance that will help you reach a decision about whether or not they have met the standards in question. Take into account who the person is and their experience or qualifications, their degree of involvement or supervision with the learner, and the nature of the evidence presented.

Activity: Checking others' suitability

It's best to identify people who may be able to give an account of the learner's performance during the assessment planning process. They should usually be people who work with the learner and who are in a position to observe their performance on a regular basis. To check that a person you have identified is suitable, ask your learner the following questions:

Questions for your learner	Yes	No
1 Can the person observe you in the workplace?	☐	☐
2 Do they work with you regularly?	☐	☐
3 Do they know the requirements of your job?	☐	☐
4 Can they comment on whether or not you are performing well?	☐	☐
5 Would they be willing to give an account of your performance?	☐	☐

You are aiming for a yes in each case, but as the assessor you have the final say in who to choose.

Briefing others

Once you've identified a suitable person, you need to brief them about what's involved. You will save time and trouble if you tell the person exactly what you want them to do beforehand, and you're more likely to get a meaningful account. Overall, you're asking them to provide an objective account of what the learner can do. This means that you will need to ask them to:

- use their own words and the active voice ('I have seen Dawn...' rather than 'It was noted…', or similar)

- be objective: sticking to what they see the learner do, rather than commenting on the kind of person they are and/or making value judgements; avoiding, for example, 'Narinder is a lovely girl and produced an excellent report.'

- describe what the learner does: the work task(s), the context and conditions, and their timescales and/or frequency, and whether this is based in the work environment

- refer to relevant records, policies and procedures, and where they are kept

- refer to the outcomes of the work the learner does (this might be a work product such as roof, a sill, a painted wall, a haircut, or a report or an invoice) and where these can be seen, if appropriate.

Ask them to sign and date their account and to give you their contact details so that you can follow it up if you need to.

The ad hoc opportunity

Other people you may come across on an ad hoc basis can form a vital part of assessment. These are the people with whom the learner comes into contact in the course of carrying out their job, such as clients, hotel guests, customers, service users and telephone callers. They can't be contacted in advance, yet if they are available on the day you assess they can corroborate what's taken place and help you reach your assessment decision. As the assessor, you need to identify appropriate opportunities within your occupational area to talk to people such as these on an ad hoc basis.

Written accounts by others

Other people's written accounts like the one shown opposite should not only provide an objective description of what the learner can do, but also be able to provide evidence towards specific learning outcomes. You can then follow up the account with other assessment methods, such as examining work products or questioning, in order to make sure that the evidence given in the account is valid, authentic and sufficient.

Tip

Once your learner understands how another person's account may be used, he or she can take advantage of any unplanned opportunities at work.

Remember

It's important for you to gain the other person's commitment, as you may be asking them to write a report, or to comment in detail.

'I make a point of asking a customer how they have been treated by the learner. You can't ask them in advance – you ask them on the spot.'

'If my learner's been working alongside someone else, I ask if I can talk to that person.'

Example of another person's account

Here's an example of a centre manager's account (witness testimony) written for a learner assessor working towards the Certificate in Assessing Vocational Achievement:

SB'S ACCOUNT OF JAMES HODSON FOR THE CERTIFICATE IN ASSESSING VOCATIONAL ACHIEVEMENT

Following our telephone conversation about James's work in our centre, I can confirm that he started work as an assessor in our centre on 1 June 2010. Since then he has participated in scheduled standardisation meetings that have included evidence from his allocated learners. Evidence of this is maintained in our centre records, and will be available to you as agreed when you visit.

I am also happy to confirm that James has consistently met the requirements of our internal quality assurance procedures. His assessments have been consistent with the assessment strategy for the qualification, and his assessment work complies with our internal assessment and internal quality assurance policies. In particular, he has used our standard documentation throughout all of his assessment work including the assessment plans, assessment records, records of reviews and records of assessment decisions and feedback. All documentation has been properly completed and appropriately filed. Sampling of his work through our internal sampling procedures has shown that in completing documentation he has created adequate audit trails that enable learner progress and achievement to be tracked from the documentation in learner portfolios back to the centre records, and vice versa.

As mentioned above, you can confirm this by examining our centre records, which will be available to you when you visit.

Finally, I can confirm that all of our centre's assessment policies and procedures in relation to health, safety and welfare have been complied with and also that our policies relating to the handling of personal data/confidentiality and equality and diversity have been complied with at all times.

I trust that the above is adequate for your needs, but if you require further information or clarification please do not hesitate to contact me.

S. Bullock,

Internal Quality Assurer and Centre Co-ordinator

14 March 2011

The statement in this paragraph helps to meet the requirements for assessment criterion 2.3 or 2.5, but doesn't provide sufficient evidence in itself: you need to examine the evidence in the workplace. This is an opportunity to combine assessment methods. While looking at the evidence in the workplace you could have a discussion with the person or the learner, or both, asking appropriate questions. Remember that when evidence is left in the workplace your assessment records must say where this is kept.

The rest of the statement also provides evidence towards several of the learning outcomes (3 and 4, for example). You would need to examine these work products to meet the requirements of other parts of the unit and, again, these could be left in the workplace and discussed with the learner and this person as necessary. This will also give you the opportunity to see how the documentation has met quality assurance requirements by asking the learner to 'walk you through' the centre's systems and procedures.

Again, remember to do this.

Here, the person confirms the learner's competence over time in areas of policy and procedures linked to all three units.

Be prepared to contact the person and question them further, even if they don't offer.

Recording another person's account

You don't always have to use a written account from the other person. Other ways of recording an account are:

- you, the assessor, questioning them and noting their answers (particularly suitable for ad hoc opportunities)

- using video, disc or internet technology such as Skype, involving the learner and with the other person's input and commentary

- writing down their account as you watch or listen to them (via the internet or over the phone). If they prefer not to take notes, they can always ring you during their observation and ask you to write down what they are seeing. You can then ask them to read through what you wrote and sign and date it if they feel it is an accurate account of what took place.

- If you haven't talked to the other person directly, be prepared to follow up their account with questioning, either face to face, via email or by phone.

Using learner statements

Learner statements can be an appropriate way of assessing learning outcomes in the affective domain, that is, to show how their attitudes have developed over time. They can also provide supplementary evidence of the learner's ability to carry out a range of activities and tasks in cases where you've asked them to keep a record of the ways in which they have done so.

Dos and dont's when using learner statements

Do	Don't
• use them with learners who are well motivated and capable	• use them on their own for assessment purposes – they are unreliable
• use them as a means of assessing: • changes in behaviour over a period of time • 'deeper' cognitive skills such as the ability to reflect and to critically evaluate	• use them for assessing performance or practical skills – there are more appropriate methods
• be prepared to teach the skills needed to produce a worthwhile account (otherwise you may set the learner up for failure)	• use written accounts with learners who have difficulty with literacy: try verbal statements instead. Remember, too, that keeping log books or diaries is time-consuming for the learner
• use blogs, particularly if learners can access them by phone	

'One big no-no is the learner writing the account and getting the other person to sign it: that's not valid. But you can get the learner to write a report and ask the person to comment on it and countersign it. That way you can check that they have read through it in detail.'

Example of a learner blog

Read through the following entries from a candidate teacher's blog, where she reflects on her teaching strategies and the ways in which she manages her learners and tries to motivate them. What do they tell you about her attitude to teaching and to her learners?

Learner blog

I have chosen two blog entries to reflect on. These are the entries that have had the most impact on my teaching practice and my confidence as a new teacher. The first explains how I attempted to use a new teaching method with a group of hairdressers. The second concerns a peer observation and describes how this has influenced the way in which I manage group behaviour.

Blog entry 1:
Trying out a new technique
What happened?

I taught my Hairdressing Year 1 students. There are eight girls ranging from Entry level 3 to Level 2.
This was my first lesson on using Excel spreadsheets.

I wanted to try something new: group work. I thought this would help students to get to know G (a new member of the group) as they always sit in the same place, next to the same people and don't talk to each other very much. They hated being split into small groups! L became aggressive and was reluctant to move. H refused to move several times and only did so when I asked her, 'Are you refusing to do the work?'

What went well/badly and how did I feel about it?

The group kept saying 'I don't know what to do,' but I had put the objectives on screen and read them out. I felt like I had failed. The session felt disorganised and unstructured.

Reflection: What are the implications?

The group didn't really work together and I admitted this to them at the end. I did try to explain why I had done it like this, but perhaps I wasn't clear enough.

On reflection, I think the group may have reacted badly to me using a new method and I should try again. Perhaps, too, I need to show the group a finished example next time, so that they can see what they are aiming for.

From reading *How Children Fail* by John Holt (1982), I have also learnt that group work can be enjoyable for some students but frightening for others. Group work means discussing things in front of others, and students are scared that this will raise questions they might not be able to answer. When they are working individually they can just do their best without anyone else challenging their choices. I can relate to how students might feel and why they might behave badly. This has helped me to empathise with students and look at ways of giving them a choice in the way they might like to learn.

Blog entry 2: Peer observation

What happened?

I have been having problems with my Year 2 Motor Vehicle apprentices who have been put on a warning by the Head of Department. I wanted to see how other teachers deal with group behaviour and arranged to observe A, a teacher in another part of the organisation.

The students were similar to mine – their behaviour was almost identical. They found it hard to keep on task and to take responsibility for their work and learning. They wanted a lot of attention from A and were not good at reading their instructions. They needed to be constantly entertained and engaged to stay motivated. The atmosphere in the classroom was also very similar to mine – relaxed, friendly, and non-threatening.

What went well/badly and how did I feel about it?

It was very interesting to see A's strategies. I have never observed a male teacher before, so I was intrigued to see if the students would react differently to him.

A ignores attention-seeking behaviour more than I would. I found this interesting to observe. The students did eventually stop trying to gain his attention, so this is something I might try. It certainly saved him a lot of effort because he wasn't wasting time keeping one person on task. I did think the one-hour lesson was too long, though. I would have given them a break after 45 minutes, as they seemed to get very chatty and distracted towards the end of the session.

This observation made me realise that the strategies I use to control behaviour are similar to A's. He does use a particular teaching method that I can see works with students – he gives them one-to-one support and sets them individual objectives. He also links every task to the students' work and embeds his teaching in what they do every day.

Reflection: What are the implications?

I recognise how much my own confidence has increased from seeing A in action. Previously I may have turned a blind eye to bad behaviour and hoped that it would not escalate, but now I feel more confident about challenging students and giving them very clear guidelines on what is and isn't acceptable.

I have learnt that providing individual support seems to be the key to ensuring that students complete their work. I have also started to design activities that are relevant to the student's workplace (such as the exercise in which I ask them to look up job advertisements on the internet and compare salaries using an Excel spreadsheet – students enjoyed this as they could see its relevance to their future).

References

Holt, J. (1982), *How Children Fail* (2nd edition), Penguin Books, London

Projects, assignments and case studies

You can use projects, assignments and case studies both for assessment purposes and to develop learners' skills, knowledge and understanding. It's important to be clear about the purpose of using each of these assessment methods and to understand the possible pitfalls, because their misuse could mean that you and your learner have wasted time on them. This chapter explains the differences between projects, assignments and case studies, when to use them, how to assess them, how to use them developmentally, and how to write a brief. It also gives examples of these types of assessment.

Definition and purpose

The following table shows the main differences between these assessment methods, and the reasons for using them.

Item	Definition	Purpose
Assignment	Assignments are problem-solving activities with a clear brief, a structured framework, guidelines on how to carry them out, a specified length (often in the form of a word count), and a time limit.	To assess in-depth knowledge and its application, for example when demonstrating generic skills such as communication or functional English; or showing evidence that the learner knows and can follow a particular procedure or process.
Project	Projects are investigations or exercises involving practical activities and tasks. They tend to be more open-ended than assignments, and can be tackled by both individual learners and groups. Learners carry them out without close supervision, although the assessor may provide guidance and support. They have a more extended timescale than assignments, although they are still time-bound.	To assess practical skills and tasks, such as in producing work products, and evidence of team working (where learners work in groups).
Case study	Case studies are illustrations or descriptions of a set of real-life circumstances or an event, followed by instructions asking learners to analyse the circumstances, draw conclusions and/or make suggestions about ways of tackling them.	To assess how the learner would apply their knowledge and skills to a specific situation.

When to use projects, assignments and case studies

Consider the following points when deciding whether to use a project, an assignment or a case study.

Assignments are good for:

- assessing learning outcomes concerned with applying practical skills and related knowledge and understanding, and for situations that involve task management and/or problem solving

- assessing whether or not learners can work within time limits

- situations where learners have to show initiative, or demonstrate that they can work without, or under limited, supervision

- covering several units and/or learning outcomes at the same time.

Don't use them...

- unless they are written at a suitable level for the learner (you aren't testing the learner's ability to read and write)

- as a way of avoiding teaching learners the generic skills they need for the world of work, such as report writing, problem solving and working with other people; learners don't learn these by osmosis.

'In instances where I have asked a learner a question during an observation and they have no idea of the answer, I may set an assignment to get them to find it out from colleagues or other sources in time for the next assessment.'

Projects are good for:

- assessment of a wide range of skills, and for integrating activities both within and across units.

- assessing learning outcomes to do with analysis, synthesis, evaluation and reflection

- learners who possess the necessary skills to carry them out successfully (such as research skills, report writing and the ability to organise themselves)

- group work, provided you are clear about who does what.

Don't use them…

- in groups to assess high-order skills (such as leadership abilities, taking the initiative and decision-making) unless you are prepared to observe

- as a short cut: practical projects are time-consuming to prepare and to assess.

Case studies are good for:

- assessing process skills such as problem solving and decision making in the work-related environment

- for situations where there are no right or wrong answers

- showing learners the relevance of a particular set of circumstances to their work environment

- introducing learners to situations they are likely to encounter in the working environment – as a development tool.

Don't use them…

- for assessment purposes as a way of saving time or avoiding the real working environment: they are not a valid means of assessing learners' performance under working conditions

- on their own for assessment purposes: they only tell you a small part of what the learner knows and understands. In addition, assessing or marking them can prove a challenge because of the range of approaches and responses that learners might give.

Assessing assignments, projects and case studies

If you use projects, assignments and/or case studies for assessment purposes, your awarding organisation will have guidance on how to structure them, and a marking or grading scheme showing you how to assess them, particularly if you are using them with learners taking higher-level qualifications.

Here are some definitions that may help you.

- **Internal assessment**
  This is where your centre sets the project, assignment and/or case study (see the example assignment specification on page 85). You may also be free to set the assessment scheme, but the awarding body will normally give clear parameters and guidance for this.

- **External assessment**
  This is where the awarding body sets the assignment and assessment scheme, and you follow it.

- **Closed assessment**
  This is where the criteria for assessing are very specific: there is only one right answer, or the learner has to give a specific example (from a list that you or the awarding body have specified) to illustrate a given point.

- **Open assessment**
  This is where there is room for the learner to demonstrate what they know in different ways, and you can use your discretion as the assessor or person marking the assignment.

Devising assessment schemes

As a team of assessors, if it is up to you to devise the assessment scheme for your project, assignment or case study, you will need to agree a detailed checklist. This checklist should include:

- the skills, knowledge and/or behaviour you want learners to demonstrate

- the condition(s) under which learners need to perform

- any degree of variation in performance that would be acceptable.

To help you define your checklist, use the learning outcomes within the units of the qualifications you are assessing, or the standards. Aim for a holistic approach and work across several units and/or learning outcomes at a time, so that you develop a checklist that integrates the standards and reflects the way in which the learner would naturally approach the task.

The facing page shows an example of an assessment specification for a Level 3 customer service assignment.

Level 3 customer service assignment

Unit ABC1: Assessment specification

This assignment must demonstrate achievement of the following learning outcomes:

1.1 Identify the main modes of communication used in the customer service environment

1.2 Explain effective face-to-face interaction, including social and environmental factors, body language and active listening

1.3 Differentiate between communication styles, to include recognition of the learner's own style of communication

1.4 Recognise ways in which emotions affect communication

1.5 Describe factors that may affect communication, including culture, age, use of language, sensory impairment, religion, and socioeconomic status

1.6 Explain the specific demands and adaptations required in telephone communication

1.7 Describe influences on relationships between members of a working team, to include perceptions, roles, expertise and responsibilities

1.8 Summarise the value of clients to the organisation within a customer service environment

1.9 Explain important customer service factors for clients, to include information, courtesy, responsiveness and presentation of the organisation

1.10 Explain the principles of handling a complaint

The learner will consider what constitutes effective communication and customer service through the exploration of specific critical incidents he or she experiences within a customer service environment using one of the following situations:

- communicating with a new client

- communicating with a difficult client

- communicating with a client in an emergency.

The learner must discuss specific examples of good practice, reflect on his or her contribution and identify areas that could benefit from improvement.

Learning providers are advised to provide a different assignment focused on one of the above options for each cohort of learners.

Learners should:

- produce a satisfactory assignment on time, using a range of study skills, reflective practices and strategies

- demonstrate that they are able to apply theory to practice

- show ability to make reference to, and apply, key texts and/or supporting literature/materials

- identify the style(s), mode(s) and model(s) of communication involved in their chosen incident

- discuss the effectiveness of communication and customer service in the chosen incident(s), and explore possible ways in which this might have been improved, if appropriate

- discuss how the role of colleagues affects how they communicate

- identify factors that may affect a client's interaction with the customer service team.

Word limit

The maximum word limit suggested by the awarding organisation for this assignment is 2,500 words (excluding references and bibliography). Learning providers must provide learners with clear guidance on the maximum length permitted and ask learners to provide a word count. Assignments that exceed the stated limit should not be accepted.

Submission

This assignment must be submitted and marks notified to the awarding organisation.

Grading

To pass, learners must achieve a minimum of 70% of available marks.

Quality assurance

Assignments will be subject to a process of independent moderation in accordance with awarding organisation guidance.

Using projects, assignments and case studies developmentally

You can use projects, assignments and case studies to develop learners' skills and knowledge. Here, you set the learning outcomes you want the learners to achieve through doing the piece of work.

A common mistake is to give all learners the same large project or assignment at the start of their learning programmes – often one that covers all units and learning outcomes – and tell them they are going to be assessed on the outcomes. Learners may find this daunting, since at this early stage of their programme they usually possess neither the occupational competence nor the problem-solving skills required to carry it out successfully.

This is where smaller projects, assignments and case studies come into their own. You can set them with a specific objective in mind, such as writing a letter of application. Only when your learner is ready to progress should you set a larger one covering several tasks or stages.

Key considerations for writing briefs

- Make sure you write a clear, specific brief saying what the project, assignment or case study is for, the objectives or outcomes the learner will achieve, and a summary of what's involved.

- Use language your learner will understand. Avoid long sentences, and address the learner directly (use 'you').

- Make links to the units and learning outcomes that the learner will be covering.

- Be clear about your aims and objectives, because if you aren't, the learner won't be either.

- Break down assignments and projects into a series of smaller steps or stages that the learner needs to complete; and give examples, prompts or pointers at each stage.

- Include the assessment criteria, simplified if necessary – these tell the learner how well they need to perform to succeed.

- Try your projects, assignments and case studies with learners, and be prepared to modify them in areas where they don't work or where learners don't perform well.

- Start with work tasks with which the learner is already familiar, and use these as the basis for your assignment or project brief. This is particularly important if you are aiming to develop generic skills such as communication or working with others, or functional skills.

How to choose a topic

One way of choosing a topic for an assignment is to start with a task the learner does as part of their day-to-day work, then to broaden it into other areas you want the learner to develop. Similarly, a project or case study should relate to an actual real-life task or scenario that the learner is likely to encounter in their workplace.

The example opposite of a health and safety assignment was used to develop learners' skills in analysing and presenting numerical data, calculating and comparing costs, and presenting findings to colleagues.

Sample developmental assignment

Assignment: What's the cost?

This assignment asks you to read and understand your organisation's health and safety policy and to consider the cost of accidents. You will need your manager or supervisor's help to obtain the policies and statistics required to carry out this assignment successfully.

Stage 1: Read your health and safety policy

Ask your manager or supervisor for a copy of the organisation's health and safety policy. Read through it and make a list of the key points it contains.

Stage 2: Analyse statistics and investigate further

Choose an aspect of health and safety that needs further investigation. Use your organisation's safety records, accident books, etc. Ask your manager for help with interpreting these if necessary. Compare accident statistics over the last five years, and choose an area that needs further investigation by answering these questions:

- Are there any trends?
- Do accidents happen at certain times of the day/month/year?
- Do the same accidents occur again and again?

Stage 3: Compare statistics and present them in chart form

Use the internet to find out how your organisation's statistics compare with those of other companies. For example, you could group statistics into types of accident and time of year when they occur. Next, choose a suitable format for representing your figures, such as a pie or bar chart.

Stage 4: Make recommendations for reducing accidents

Discuss ways of reducing accidents with your manager or supervisor, and turn these into proposals for your organisation. Do this by listing the steps that the organisation would need to take, and any resources needed.

Stage 5: Calculate the costs

Choose one area where accidents occur, and work out how much it would cost your organisation to implement your suggested proposals. Now calculate what accidents already cost your organisation in lost time, staff absence, sick pay, etc. Compare your costs with these.

Stage 6: Present your findings

Give a five-minute talk to management and colleagues on your proposals. Prepare Powerpoint slides and notes to help you make your main points. Make sure you explain the comparative costs.

Stage 7: Assess your performance

Think about how well you completed this assignment:

- What did you do well?
- Was there anything you found challenging? If so, what?
- What would you do differently next time?

Sample case study

Consider the following scenario:

Just before lunchtime, a number of pallets of waste are delivered to site. The forklift truck driver, responsible for unloading and moving the wastes to the correct storage area, is due to finish soon as he has the afternoon off, but says he will 'sort it out' before he goes.

About five minutes later the supervisor hears a loud bang and, on coming out of his office, sees that a stack of palletised wastes has collapsed and is spread across the store. Fortunately, the wastes are still intact and no one has been injured. It later transpires that the operative was taking a shortcut and travelling at speed through a narrow gap meant for pedestrian access. He had clipped the edge of a pallet, causing the stack to topple over. He claimed that he had never been told that he couldn't drive there and that he hadn't had any

training. The supervisor said he had personally inducted him when he started with the company, four years earlier, and part of the induction included health and safety training.

i How do you minimise the risk of this sort of accident happening on your site?

ii How would you deal with the operative if this accident had happened on your site? Explain the procedures you would follow.

iii Suppose this accident had happened on your site, resulting in someone being badly injured and a subsequent investigation by outside agencies. How would you demonstrate to them that you have effective procedures in place and that all operatives have been trained, and understand them?

iv What additional records would have to be completed in the above situation (iii)?

If you are planning to use projects or assignments, it's important to know why you're using them. Use the activity below to help you decide.

Activity: *Should I use a project, assignment or case study?*

Answer the following questions and use the feedback below to help you establish your main purpose.

Questions	Yes	No
1 Is it to help the learner apply and develop the skills in which they will need to demonstrate competence?	☐	☐
2 Is it to assess learners' ability and how they apply knowledge?	☐	☐
3 Is it so that a cohort of learners can generate evidence to cover the standards?	☐	☐

If you have answered yes to 1, then a project, assignment and/or case study can be a helpful way of achieving this.

If, however, you have answered yes to 2 or 3, consider the following:

Evidence against the standards must be individual to each learner. You can't give all your learners the same project or assignment for them to demonstrate their individual knowledge and ability. Instead, projects should come from everyday, naturally occurring work activities. You should plan for this using a variety of more appropriate assessment methods, including observation, evidence from others, examination of products and discussion or questioning.

If you already do all of these, ask yourself why you need a project or assignment too.

Other assessment methods

If it is difficult or impossible to obtain performance evidence from the workplace environment, you may need to use simulation as an assessment method instead, in order to be able to observe what a learner can do. Simulation is not strictly an assessment method: it's the creation of an environment that's as close to the learner's real working conditions as possible.

Some but not all learning programmes include a requirement to take tests in core skills. These are supervised tests that are assessed by the awarding organisation. However, the new functional skills offer a range of different opportunities, and awarding organisations are offering a wider choice of assessment approach to these.

Using written questions may also sometimes be a valid assessment method in certain circumstances.

This chapter tells you how and when to use:

- simulation

- skills testing

- written questions in the working environment.

Simulation

Simulation is only used when it's impossible for the learner to perform in a real-life situation, as, for example, when there are issues of cost, confidentiality, privacy, sensitivity or safety, or (as in the quoted examples on the right) when it's unfeasible.

Simulation can include the use of realistic work environments within the college setting, such as hairdressing salons, workshops or restaurants. However, you must comply with the strict regulations about these simulated environments as set out in the relevant assessment strategy or by your awarding organisation.

Here's an extract from the assessment strategy for firefighting and some of the standards they relate to. You will see the reasons for using a simulated environment when you read through the units.

'When you're assessing first aid, you can't resuscitate a live person.'

'There's never a shoplifter around on the shop floor when you need one.'

Firefighting

All approved centres have to meet the following principles:

Simulation must:

- include a comprehensive range of demands, activities and constraints relevant to those that would be met in a real working context

- provide individuals with access to the normal facilities, support and advice that would be available in the context and type of working situation

- ensure that formative assessment and advice are available from people with current experience of work being undertaken

- realistically reflect normal contexts and conditions

- place individuals under pressure of time, resources and working demands that would operate in a normal working environment

- be used in accordance with guidelines at unit level within the qualification

- be planned, developed and documented by the centre in a way that ensures that simulations correctly reflect what the standard seeks to assess (validity).

In addition:

- a centre's overall strategy for simulation must be examined and approved by the awarding body's external verifier

- there should be a number of different simulations to cover the same aspect of standards in order to reduce the risk of collusion.

Units

FF3: Save and preserve endangered life	FF4: Resolve operational incidents	FF5: Protect the environment from the effects of hazardous materials
FF3.1 Conduct a search to locate life involved in incidents	FF4.1 Control and extinguish fires	FF5.1 Mitigate damage to the environment from hazardous materials
FF3.2 Rescue life involved in incidents	FF4.2 Resolve incidents other than those involving a fire or hazardous materials	FF5.2 Decontaminate people and property affected by hazardous materials
FF3.3 Provide treatment to casualties	FF4.3 Support people involved in an operational incident	FF5.3 Support people involved in hazardous materials incidents
FF3.4 Support people involved in rescue operations		

Making the most of simulation

Successful simulations take a great deal of planning and preparation. They are only worth doing if you have sufficient time and resources, otherwise they will not produce the performance evidence you need. Many centres that have formed partnerships with local employers make arrangements to use their premises to provide the real work environment, while in return they provide assessment services to the employers.

When you assess learners in a simulated environment, you still use the main assessment methods, just as you would when assessing under real working conditions. Conditions may be simulated, but the assessment is real.

Recording your results

Although you will be using observation during the simulation itself, you need to concentrate on the areas that differ significantly from reality, and address these using a combination of the main assessment methods. These methods include:

- observing your learner carrying out the simulated activity and then assessing any products that emerge from this

- using another's account (witness testimony), particularly if the person in question has seen the learner perform in the real workplace

- questioning the learner before, during or immediately after the simulation: asking them how they would act under different circumstances, for example

- holding a discussion, where the learner brings along products to support their claim to competence.

You need to reach your assessment decision using VAS, and record your decision as you would when carrying out any observation.

Skills tests

Some qualifications contain an element of skills testing, where skills are part of the overall qualification requirements. Others, such as apprenticeship frameworks, require learners to achieve specific qualifications that require testing, such as functional skills. In these cases, you will be required to implement the testing as stipulated by your awarding organisation.

Functional skills

Functional skills are qualifications at various levels that develop the essential literacy, numeracy and ICT skills necessary to 'function' in work, learning and life. The functional skills replace the three key skills of Communication, Application of Number and ICT, and form part of all 14–19 and adult learning pathways in England. The three functional skills are in:

- Mathematics

- ICT

- English, which has three components: speaking, listening and communication; reading; and writing.

Here is an example of part of an online skills test for functional English in reading at Level 2, where learners are being asked to compare texts:

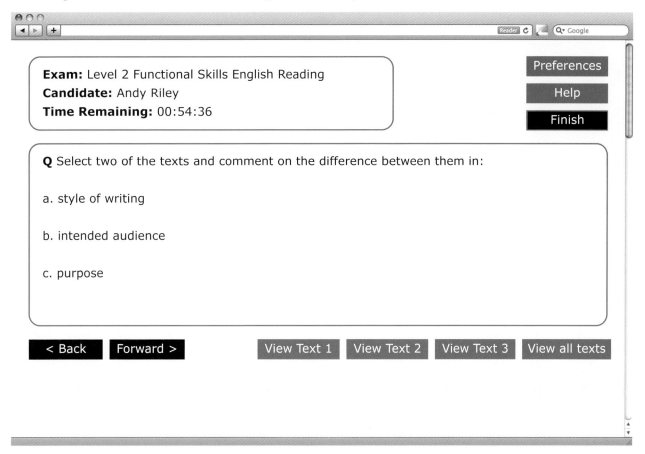

To pass functional skills in mathematics, ICT, and the reading and writing components of English, learners have to take an assessment that is externally set and marked by the awarding organisation. For the speaking, listening and communication component, centres are allowed to set internal assessment, following strict criteria set by the awarding organisations in:

- how tasks are set
- the ways in which learners can tackle them
- task marking.

Preparing for tests

If your centre uses testing, you will need procedures in place for both preparing learners and managing the tests.

Preparing learners

- Make sure that learners are ready to be entered for the test (otherwise you are setting them up for failure).
- Help learners acquire test techniques, such as knowing how to deal with online or multi-choice questions.
- Allow them to practise under test conditions, using appropriate equipment and timing them.

Managing the tests

- Ensure the security of test papers: for example, you'll need procedures in place for receiving, storing and returning completed papers, if you use these.

- Have procedures for dealing with learners with particular requirements. For example, you might need to allow a learner with a physical disability to take a supervised rest period. Your awarding organisation will have guidelines.

- Have enough trained staff in place to administer and invigilate, and to be on hand in case of emergencies during the test.

- Communicate results and send certificates out to learners. (There's often a delay between the test result and receiving the certificate, so it's important not to lose touch with the learner during this time.)

Using written questions in the workplace

Some assessment strategies allow you to use written questions. These can be useful if time is of the essence and/or you have learners spread over a wide geographical area. However, giving a written set of questions to all learners as a matter of course is poor practice. Preprepared questions take no account of the learner's particular circumstances and knowledge. They might also disadvantage learners whose literacy levels are low. Written questions should therefore be as individual as the learner and their circumstances. As an assessment method, you should use written questions for learners to show their knowledge only if it has not been demonstrated or proved in other ways.

Recognising prior learning

If you are responsible for assessing qualifications that come under the Qualifications and Credit Framework (QCF), you need to know about recognition of prior learning (RPL). The QCF offers scope to personalise learning, and as a result RPL is now high on the agenda. The QCF aims to widen access and create additional opportunities for recognising individual achievement and simplifying the way in which this happens. A learner can match what they have already learned to individual units in QCF qualifications, and be awarded credit for achieving these units as a result of undergoing the RPL process.

RPL in the QCF is defined as:

'A method of assessment that considers whether a learner can demonstrate that they can meet the requirements of a unit through knowledge, understanding and skills they already possess and do not need to develop through a course of learning.'[1]

This section explains the six stages of the RPL process.

1 *Claiming credit: Guidance on the recognition of prior learning within the Qualifications and Credit Framework*, QCDA, 2010.

The RPL process

Not all learners have access to formal programmes of learning, so centres need a process of RPL that is responsive to their needs and opens up their access to a wider range of assessment instruments and methods. The learner is at the centre of the RPL process, and decides whether or not to claim credit using this route. Your centre's job is to provide advice, guidance and support to enable learners to make the right choice about whether or not to take the RPL route, and if they do, to assess, IQA and certificate their evidence as appropriate.

This is where you come in as the assessor. Where the learner chooses to claim credit using the RPL route, you will assess whether or not their evidence meets the standards they are claiming credit for, using the assessment methods and processes you would normally use. Depending on your centre's procedures, you may also be involved in assessment planning and supporting learners through the RPL process.

Remember

One of the main principles of RPL is that peoples' prior achievements can now be recognised, and learners don't have to repeat learning unnecessarily.

The stages in the RPL process

All centres offering qualifications under the QCF need the following RPL process in place. Here are the stages involved:

Stage 1	Stage 2	Stage 3
General information, advice and guidance (IAG) about claiming credit	**Pre-assessment – gathering evidence and giving information**	**Assessment/ documentation of evidence**
The learner is given information, advice and guidance about the process for claiming credit to make a decision about whether or not to use the RPL route. This includes administration processes, sources of professional support and guidance, timelines, appeals, and any fees and/or subsidies available.	Once the learner decides to claim credit through RPL, they must collect evidence against the requirements of the unit(s). This may involve having an assessment plan or choosing other means of supporting their claim. The learner needs to be aware of the implications of the process, have sufficient support to make a viable claim and be able to make decisions about how to collect and present evidence against the learning objectives and assessment criteria.	When you assess evidence as part of RPL, you follow a structured process for gathering and reviewing the evidence and making judgments about the learner's prior learning and experience in relation to unit standards. In other words, you use the same process for reaching an assessment decision as you would for any other learner.

Exemptions and credit transfer

Exemption and credit transfer are two other processes that support RPL under the QCF, but they are not the same as RPL.

Exemption is where a learner claims exemption from some of the achievement requirements of a QCF qualification using evidence of certificated, non-QCF achievement deemed to be of equivalent value.

Credit transfer refers to the process of transferring credits from one unit/qualification across to another for certification purposes.

Key point

RPL is a robust process where the learner's evidence behind their claim for credit is assessed in the same way as all other evidence, using valid and reliable methods. On occasions it may be simpler to assess current evidence, for example by observing the learner performing tasks in real time.

...age 4 ...edback	Stage 5 Awarding credit	Stage 6 Appealing
...er assessment, you discuss the ...ults with the learner and confirm ...ether or not you recommend ...t credits be awarded following ...r centre's normal procedures. ...this point you would need to give ...port and guidance on the options ...ilable, including further learning ...development (particularly in ...es where your recommendation ...ot to award credit).	All credits achieved through RPL are recorded in the personal learning record by the awarding organisation in exactly the same way as all other credits.	Learners who wish to appeal against an assessment decision follow your centre's standard appeals procedure.

What the standards say

National occupational standards (NOS) Standard 9: Assess learner achievement	
Performance criteria	**Knowledge and understanding**
9.3 Use valid, fair, reliable and safe assessment methods	**KU11** How to determine when evidence is sufficient to make an assessment decision
9.4 Identify and collect evidence that is valid, authentic and sufficient	**KU12** How to judge the authenticity and currency of evidence and what to do when there is doubt

Assessor units		
Unit title	**Learning outcomes**	**Assessment criteria**
1 Understanding the principles and practices of assessment	**2** Understand different types of assessment methods **5** Understand how to make assessment decisions	
2 Assess occupational competence in the work environment	**2** Be able to make assessment decisions about occupational competence	**2.1** Use valid, fair and reliable assessment methods including: • observation of performance • examining products of work • questioning the learner • discussion with the learner • use of others (witness testimony) • looking at learner statements • recognising prior learning
3 Assess vocational skills, knowledge and understanding	**2** Be able to carry out assessments of vocational skills, knowledge and understanding	**1.1** Select methods to assess vocational skills, knowledge and understanding which address learner needs and meet assessment requirements including: • assessments of the learner in simulated environments • skills tests • oral and written questions • assignments • projects • case studies • recognising prior learning